Writing better requirements

Ian F. Alexander and Richard Stevens

Addison-Wesley

An imprint of **PEARSON EDUCATION**

London ■ New York ■ Toronto ■ Sydney ■ Tokyo ■ Singapore ■ Hong Kong
Cape Town ■ New Delhi ■ Madrid ■ Paris ■ Amsterdam ■ Munich ■ Milan

PEARSON EDUCATION LIMITED

Edinburgh Gate
Harlow CM20 2JE
Tel: +44 (0)1279 623623
Fax: +44 (0)1279 431059

www.pearson.com

First published in Great Britain in 2002

ISBN-10: 0-321-13163-0
ISBN-13: 978-0-321-13163-8

British Library Cataloguing in Publication Data
A CIP catalogue record for this book can be obtained from the British Library

Library of Congress Cataloging-in-Publication Data

Alexander, Ian (Ian F.), 1954-
    Writing better requirements / Ian Alexander and Richard Stevens.
        p. cm.
    Includes bibliographical references and index.
    ISBN 0-321-13163-0 (pbk. : alk. paper)
      1. Software engineering. 2. Systems engineering. I. Stevens, Richard, 1946- II. Title.

    QA76.758 .A43 2002
    005.1--dc21

                                                    2002071110

10 9 8 7 6

Designed by Sue Lamble
Typeset by Pantek Arts Ltd, Maidstone, Kent
Printed and bound in Great Britain by Bell and Bain Ltd, Glasgow

The Publishers' policy is to use paper manufactured from sustainable forests.

...uucestershire GL50 2RH
Telephone: 01242 714333

Writing better requirements

Contents

1 Introduction

2 Identifying the stakeholders

3 Gathering requirements from stakeholders

7   Requirements writing   96

8   Checking and reviewing   108

Foreword

Why do requirements matter? Experience has shown that insufficient attention is paid to requirements. The price paid for this lack of focus and applied practices is systems that don't meet customer needs; take longer to develop than planned; and cost more than customers are willing to pay.

Are we ready to change? Are you willing to spend some time and effort involved in practical exercises to experience how better requirements should evolve? If yes, commit to digesting the counsel of two experienced practitioners and to changing current practices to ones that will produce better results.

Alexander and Stevens have described how to identify stakeholders and capture requirements, how to write good requirements, how to structure and organize requirements for system developers, and how to review requirements informally and formally. They have provided a set of useful references to further support your efforts.

Experience has shown us that investment in the requirements process saves time, money, and effort. Yet, development efforts consistently charge ahead without investing sufficiently in the requirements process. We are so intent to develop the technical solutions that we are unwilling to take the time and effort to understand and meet the *real* customer needs.

Gathering requirements is the most critical activity in providing a new system or capability. How many of us are willing to invest the time, effort, and money in identifying the real customer needs before we start off spending technical resources in developing a system? The pressure to start writing code and produce "working" software is great – accentuated by our managers' quest for "results" and everyone "being busy!"

Ian Alexander and Richard Stevens are interested in helping you to evolve requirements that meet real customer needs. They have provided an approach that is based on experience and lessons learned from decades in "the school of practical experience."

Your software and system development efforts and activities will benefit from their advice. Take the time to digest their sage advice and make the effort to respond to the exercises. Apply these concepts and lessons to your own development efforts.

In short, Ian Alexander and Richard Stevens have provided a practical guide for those who endeavor to satisfy customers.

Dr. Ralph R. Young
Practitioner and Author

Preface

It isn't that they can't see the solution.
It is that they can't see the problem.

G. K. Chesterton, *The Point of a Pin* in *The Scandal of Father Brown*

Requirements are essential

Requirements are the key to project success. We all know this, but we often forget – and pay the price. Many projects, both in industry and in the public sector, fail to do what is needed. They deliver late, over budget, and with poor quality. Missing out on requirements is disastrous.

Who this book is for

Writing Better Requirements is designed as a short, convenient overview for practicing systems engineers and others who find they need to write requirements. Because it is about practical techniques, it should be useful in many different kinds of system and software projects. We aim to enable readers to write requirements which are good enough for successful systems to be specified, designed, and tested against them.

This book should also form a useful introduction for students who want to learn how to get started with requirements.

What this book does and does not cover

This book specifically focusses on how to discover and express requirements. It is not about system specification, nor how to make a design that meets user needs, nor even about how users should ensure their requirements are met.

Since users own the requirements, these must be expressed in a way users can understand. This book treats requirements as simple pieces of text, supported by operational scenarios and informal diagrams. Many attempts have been made to improve on these simple means, using more formal structures and notations, with varying success. We have not tried to cover all these approaches.

To place requirements in context, the book must of course cover some aspects of the development process. Project management, verification, quality assurance, and the development life cycle are all closely linked with requirements – indeed, each of these areas is meaningless in isolation. But in this book, we concentrate on the tasks of capturing and writing requirements. Each chapter contains exercises to help readers to practice their skills. We recommend some good books for readers who want to go beyond writing good requirements to other aspects of systems and requirements engineering.

Getting the best from this book

This book is meant to be read in the order in which it is written, taking the reader through a disciplined process of identifying, gathering, organizing, and reviewing. This is vital for success. Each chapter introduces a stage in the requirements process. Key terms are defined informally, explained, and illustrated with examples and exercises to develop the practical skills of good requirements writing. These skills involve looking at problems, dealing with people, looking critically at what is being written, and reviewing requirements effectively. Reviewing is to some extent a separate skill and can be looked at separately; the others belong together in a more or less strict sequence.

Structure of this book

We begin by illustrating the importance of requirements. You may need this chapter to convince other people that they have a problem. Too many projects have poor requirements, and never recover. If you are already convinced, you can skip this introductory chapter.

We then show in a non-technical way how to define a problem, in close co-operation with the only people who know what the problem is, the users. The body of the book steps through the process, looking at:

- how to capture requirements from users;
- how to organize these into a clear message from users to developers;
- techniques for the special kind of writing needed for requirements;
- how to review requirements informally at every stage, then formally.

Practical exercises

All the chapters in the body of the book contain practical exercises for the reader. These are designed to take about half an hour each. Some are sufficiently open-ended for more extended self-instruction, or student projects. We recommend that readers attempt each exercise, at least briefly, to get a feeling for the difficulties involved. At the back of the book are short answers to all the questions, with hints to the reader for more complete projects.

Problems before solutions

If the message of this book can be stated in a sentence, it is:

Get agreement on what people want before attempting to create solutions.

Finding out what is needed, instead of rushing into presumed solutions, is the key to every aspect of system development. Most technical problems can be solved, given determination, patience, a skilled team – and a good definition of the problem to be solved.

Acknowledgments

We would like to thank the anonymous reviewers who checked the book so carefully; our wives and families for tolerating us while we wrote; and all our consultancy, training, and workshop clients who experienced the material first-hand and showed us the way it needed to be explained. We are specially grateful to Richard Marshall for reading an early draft, and to Professor Ken Jackson for his perceptive and precise comments.

We are grateful to the following for permission to reproduce copyright material:

G.K. Chesterton quote reprinted by permission of A.P. Watt Ltd on behalf of the Royal Literary Fund.

Figure 2.1 reprinted by permission of Beccy Blake.

Figures 4.1, 6.2, and 6.4 reprinted by permission of Telelogic DOORS UK Ltd.

Table 1.1 reprinted by permission of the Standish Group International, Inc.

Introduction

This chapter explains why requirements are important and why they are often not done well, describing some of the challenges that lie ahead. The requirements process is sketched in outline, and the principal terms used in the book are introduced.

1.1 Why do requirements matter?

Requirements are crucial to every project

Every project succeeds or fails on the quality of its requirements. They set the scope of all subsequent work and tell the project team what the users want. Without good requirements, projects fail, are late, come in over budget, or produce systems that are never used.

Requirement issues should be fixed early, before committing to a design, because problems caused by poor requirements tend to be deeply embedded in the design and are difficult to remedy afterwards.

Requirements are the part that developers miss most easily

Developers have a different perspective from users as they are looking at a requirement from the point of view of how to implement it rather than experiencing the problem that the users had in the first place. The safest way to ensure that the users' needs are met is to write down, as two separate documents, what the users need, and what a system would have to do to meet that need. These are the user requirements and the system specifications respectively.

In this book we mostly discuss the simplest case – a new user problem leads to a new system specification. In reality, systems often replace or extend older systems, so requirements are often written as changes or extensions to an existing situation. "Pure" user requirements tend to be combined with design constraints from the existing systems that the new system will have to live with. This is more awkward as the requirements will be incomplete and unbalanced. However, it may still be worth writing a complete problem description, at least at high level, to provide a context for the requirements.

Doing requirements well takes time, effort, and skill at the start of a project, but saves much more time later. This book concentrates on user requirements, though the skills of clear writing will be helpful for specifying systems as well. User requirements represent the client's viewpoint, which will otherwise not be heard by developers.

Why do you need good requirements?

Snowballing cost of early mistakes

Any mistake made early in a project has consequences which snowball. Requirements are cheap to change while they are being worked on. A quick discussion, a small amount of editing, and the problem is fixed. If an error is allowed to propagate into design, the cost of correction is much larger. If system designers reach for the wrong goal, everything they do will be wrong. A single wrong requirement is likely to create a shower of design mistakes.

The worst time to try to correct a poor requirement is when a system is in operation, or a mass-market product has been released. For example, the only means open to a car maker to replace a switch or to change the firmware is to recall the cars for modification. When a mistake has been replicated in 100,000 cars, there is a severe penalty in time, effort, and damage to the company's reputation.

High price of failure

Table 1.1 lists the main causes of software project failure in a now-classic study: the ultimate price of not getting requirements right. Even if projects do not actually fail, lack of control is felt as budgets and timescales expand while functionality is lost.

TABLE 1.1 ■ Reasons for project failure

Incomplete requirements	13.1%
Didn't involve users	12.4%
Insufficient resources/schedule	10.6%
Unrealistic expectations	9.9%
Lack of managerial support	9.3%
Changing requirements	8.7%
Poor planning	8.1%
Didn't need it any longer	7.4%

Source: Standish Group 1995 (www.standishgroup.com)

Some people argue that software and systems are different, but every large software project involves hardware, networks, people, and procedures to follow: in other words, systems of a kind. In any case, the lessons about requirements and management seem to apply equally well to both system and software projects; and software is an important part of almost all modern systems. This book is not about software as such, although it will usually be present in the systems resulting from your requirements.

Five of the eight major reasons for failure are requirements-based. The other three relate to management, while – perhaps surprisingly – none of them is technical. Even systems which work are useless if they are too late, or too expensive to be completed. Stakeholders will not be happy if their systems cost a fortune, perform poorly, or are unreliable. The same is true for stock control, aircraft development, information systems or financial software. Every one of these areas has had successive failures through poor handling of requirements.

A more recent survey (*IEE Review*, July 1999) asked project managers about the causes of project difficulties: only 22 percent of them identified requirements as at all important. The difference between the two surveys may mean that management awareness of requirements needs to be raised.

The time to get requirements to a good level of quality is when they are defined: they drive everything that happens later in your project. Discovering what is really wanted may involve considerable effort, such as building prototypes to show users what they might get. This effort is repaid by the smooth running of the development project and the easy acceptance of the product.

What are requirements for?

To show what results stakeholders want

The first job of requirements is to show what results stakeholders want. They must be documented, or everyone will have different and possibly shifting views of the project's scope and objectives.

To give stakeholders a chance to say what they want

All the stakeholders in a project, whether users or not, have requirements. They use them to see what the overall project is for, and where their own work fits in. If a project is not too big, and is run as a close partnership between stakeholders and developers, detailed written requirements may not seem so important. But requirements are often the only chance that users have to tell the world what they want.

To represent different viewpoints

On a big project, different stakeholders contribute requirements from separate viewpoints. The stakeholders in a civil aircraft include users such as passengers, pilots and aircrew, baggage handlers, refueling staff, air traffic controllers, mechanics, and safety inspectors. Also to be included are managers, shareholders, and regulators like the aviation authorities: these people are not users, but they do have an interest in the project.

Different groups have their own needs, which may sometimes conflict. For example, a baggage handler wants a large cargo door, with a flat cargo area inside. The pilot wants a stable aircraft that responds smoothly to the controls. The aircraft designer will have to find a way of providing a large door without affecting the plane's handling in the air.

Where you find different viewpoints on a particular requirement, you should record them and keep them attached to the requirement, to allow the stakeholders to evaluate them. The handling of conflicts is an important but complex question which this book does not attempt to answer in detail.

To check the design

Writing down each requirement lets test engineers check that the system, as built, does what it should: they can test each part of the design and each function separately. From the developers' viewpoint, this translates to what the designed system has to do. Developers can tune a design to make it fit the need better.

To measure progress

From the development project manager's point of view, a clear requirement means that progress can be measured and areas needing attention can be identified. When it comes to meeting the customer, everyone can be confident that the project is on track, because they can see how much of the job is done already, and that it has all gone well so far.

To accept products against precise criteria

From the test engineer's point of view, a requirement is both something to be tested, and a source of acceptance criteria. Meeting these criteria provides evidence that a product does what it should. Good, sharp acceptance criteria come naturally from precise and well-organized requirement statements.

Requirements, then, are used for many different reasons by different people. For example:

- users say and get what they want;
- systems engineers can be sure they are solving the right problems;
- test engineers know what to test;
- managers have more confidence that the project is on track.

1.2 Who are requirements for?

What is a user?

A **user** is someone involved in using a system when it is actually working. Using does not only mean operating a system; testing, maintaining, and checking safety during system operation are all uses, but a safety inspector is certainly not an operator.

What is a developer?

A **developer** is someone who is involved in developing a system to satisfy the user requirements. This means anyone in a development organization; when we want to indicate more specifically which kind of developer, we use the following terms:

- **systems engineer** – someone who specifies and designs a system as a whole, as opposed to components of that system. Note that a programmer working on a software module within a system, for example, is not necessarily also a systems engineer;

- **system designer** – someone who designs a system, not necessarily software;

- **programmer** – someone who designs and writes software;

- **test engineer** – someone who tests a system, including specifying and designing any test harness that may be necessary.

What is a requirements engineer?

A **requirements engineer** is someone who helps to formulate the user requirements through all the stages described in this book. The role is essentially to facilitate the communication between the other groups, using a range of techniques to encourage open and informed dialog.

Incidentally, the requirements engineer is not necessarily a developer, and indeed may work independently or for a user organization. In the case of mass-market products such as mobile telephones or business accounting packages, the development organization may employ its own requirements engineers. They help to capture user requirements from potential or actual customers, who are represented within the organization by the marketing function.

What is a stakeholder?

A **stakeholder** is someone who has a justifiable claim to be allowed to influence the requirements. Users are nearly always stakeholders. Other stakeholders may include:

- people whose lives are affected by the system, such as clients and suppliers;

- managers who are concerned for the system to succeed, although they do not use it as such;

- regulators such as local and state governments and standards bodies, which are concerned about the effects the system may have in its environment.

People in the development organization may be stakeholders if they are responsible for the safe and continued operation of the system, or for its maintenance. A user organization is wise to involve its developers in this way.

Referring to stakeholder groups

As it is awkward to keep referring to "users and any other relevant stakeholders," we often simply say "users," even though the views of non-user stakeholders may need to be considered.

Example: window-cleaners and office workers

For example, many tall buildings are equipped with small gantries and winches to allow window-cleaners access to the myriad windows, high above the street. The office workers inside are using the building as their office; the window-cleaners are using the gantries and winches to help them maintain the building. The safety inspector is concerned that the equipment is properly constructed and maintained, and suitable for its purpose. The needs of all the different kinds of stakeholder combine to shape the system.

What is a customer?

A **customer** is someone who pays for a system development, including the requirements. Customers are usually managers rather than users, although they might be both, as in the case of a management information system. Their stake in the system involves their reputation within their own organization, the efficient running of their department, and possibly other factors such as the morale of their workforce – which may depend on having good systems. The customer may limit the scope of the user requirements, deciding through dialog with the developers what can be built within the budget available.

Note that we also refer in the ordinary sense to the people who use the services provided by, say, a bank as the bank's customers. These people could alternatively be described (from the point of view of the bank) as users of automatic teller machines or stakeholders in the bank's continued success.

1.3 Different names for requirements

Many different words are used to describe requirements, and the same words sometimes take on different meanings. In this section we establish some practical definitions for use in this book.

A **requirement** is a statement of need, something that some class of user or other stakeholder wants. Since requirements are owned by users, this book argues that the heart of each requirement should be a simple piece of natural language text. There are good reasons for supporting this text with scenarios, diagrams, status attributes, performance targets, and other values. There are in other words many requirements-on-requirements, and on projects of any size these call for tool support. The complexity must not detract from the basic need, which is for requirements to communicate users' needs clearly and accurately.

Requirements in industrial and commercial usage are typically included in contracts and therefore have legal force. In an ideal world, this would be the only meaning of "requirement," but as the term is in wide use with a range of other meanings, other more specific words are needed.

A **function** is something that a system or subsystem does, presumably because a requirement made it necessary. In a perfect world, it would be best to use this term only in system and subsystem specifications. The term is becoming less popular because of its association with structured analysis and design, as opposed to the newer object-oriented approach.

A **system function** is the same as a *function*. System functions and system constraints should not be included in user requirements documents.

A **"functional requirement"** sounds like an oxymoron – both part of a solution and part of a problem: a system specification and a user requirement? – but in practice it usually just means the same as *function*. It is not a good term but it is in wide use.

A **constraint** is a statement of restriction, modifying a requirement or set of requirements by limiting the range of acceptable solutions. Constraints govern qualities such as safety, dependability, and performance. An older but possibly misleading synonym for constraint is "non-functional requirement."

A **capability**, in a system specification, is a *function* that a system is capable of but strictly performs only when requested to by a user or another system. Functions not exposed to agents outside the system are not capabilities. However, the term is often used loosely to mean no more than "system function." In *user requirements*, a capability means something a user wants to be able to do, so in this sense it is a synonym for *affordance*.

An **affordance** – a sharper but more academic concept – is a *requirement* that affords an option or freedom to a user, whether or not the user chooses to exploit it. In *user requirements*, an affordance is any requirement except a *constraint*, whereas in system specifications relatively few requirements directly afford anything to the user. In user requirements, affordances appear in phrases such as "The operator shall be able to…" or "The operator chooses… ."

In software systems, affordances are normally exposed in a user interface; in hardware systems, affordances are exposed with controls such as levers and switches.

"Affordance" has precisely the meaning we want to distinguish user requirements that are not constraints: a **"user requirement"** is either an *affordance* or a user-imposed *constraint*. However, rather than trying to force people into using the less common term affordance, we will generally follow conventional usage and refer to user requirements that are not constraints as *capabilities*, or simply as *requirements*. A **"system requirement"** is either a *system function* or a *system constraint*, forming part of a *system specification*. The difference between user and system requirements is explained further in the next section.

1.4 Different types of specification

Different kinds of specification are needed at different stages of a project. In this book we are concerned with user requirements: defining what users and other stakeholders want. Users mainly want specific results, so they tend to write mostly **capabilities** – strictly, **affordances** that are later implemented as **system functions**. Other stakeholders such as managers and regulators are concerned with cost, technical aspects of safety, or other qualities, so they tend to write **constraints**. Users can contribute end-to-end constraints, such as desired performance and availability levels, but they shouldn't be saying how these are to be attained – that is not their business.

Later in a project, you will need system and test specifications to define what the system must do and how it is to be verified. The system design has to meet its specification, as demonstrated by passing its tests. If the project is large enough, you will use the design to identify subsystems. Each subsystem has its own set of specifications and tests; if it has a user interface it may introduce its own additional – local – user requirements. This hierarchical systems engineering approach is described in detail in Stevens *et al.*, 1998. System specification is not discussed further in this book.

User constraints

As well as defining the results that they want, users constrain system quality with requirements such as *"The vehicle shall be legal in the USA"* or *"Customers can access electronic bank facilities 24 hours per day, 7 days per week."*

These are examples of **user constraints** on the capabilities (affordances) already demanded. The constraints form part of the user requirements.

System constraints do not belong in user requirements

Later in the project, other constraints are imposed by the developers, to ensure that the delivered system will meet professional standards of quality. The various technical disciplines on the project each put their own limits on how the results are to be delivered. For example:

- the **materials engineer** may insist that beryllium (a dangerous metal) is not used in a structure.

- the **software maintenance manager** could demand that the code be written in C++ for compatibility with other work in the maintenance department.

- the **quality manager** can require compliance with international standards for system engineering.

These are system constraints, limiting the way the system can be designed and constructed. People could argue that these are not user requirements but belong in the system's specification. Against this, users can reasonably demand that they will not be exposed to poisoning, that their maintenance staff will be able to maintain their systems, and that the work that is done will be of good quality.

Constraints: costs and benefits

Constraints can help projects work smoothly, or make them impossible. They add to what has to be checked – a single requirement for safety or reliability can enormously increase the cost and complexity of a system. But without these requirements, the system may risk catastrophic failure.

1.5 The challenge of writing better requirements

The challenge in writing requirements is mainly to communicate reliably between groups of people who may never meet, and who have quite different viewpoints. For example, it may be difficult for subsystem contractors to meet users: their direct customer is the system contractor. Traditionally, a written contract, containing requirements in a technical annex, was the only means by which developers could learn what was wanted. At times this must have seemed a narrow and uncertain bridge over a deep chasm.

Cross some rivers

There are perhaps several rivers to cross, not only one, as there are various groups of people who need to communicate to make a new product a success. Here are some of the gulfs to be bridged.

Gulf between development and marketing in product companies

Most companies are good technically – they have skilled people who enjoy doing the work. The typical organization knows its technical domain well: it understands how to devise solutions to complex problems, such as database design, network integration, or integrated circuit design. In contrast, requirements may not exist at all, or are disorganized, incomplete, and full of design details. There is often a gulf between the marketing and the development arms of product companies.

To bridge the gulf, marketing has to act like the users it represents: it has to take active ownership of the user requirements. Marketing must interact intensively with development to make sure that the requirements are realistic, and with both development and management to ensure that sufficient resources are available. The outcome is a compromise acceptable to the users.

Gulf between users and developers

Users looking for a better system are in a difficult situation. They want to go on doing their business as usual – only more easily. They want things to get better, and they want to be able to forget about the problem that is bothering them.

Developers have an entirely different view, thinking about the technology, and seeing an opportunity for interesting work. They know it will take time, and they have to find out what the problem is in order to solve it properly.

A huge gulf often exists between developers and users. Each side has to understand the world of the other – and the sides must meet in the middle. Requirements are the bridge, telling the developers what the users want, and letting the users and other stakeholders control what the developers will produce. In the middle, the requirements have to be clear so that both groups understand them – in the same way.

Gulf between staff and customers

Everyone has heard teachers saying only half in jest how much more peaceful their colleges would be without students, but satisfying those people is the reason their organization exists. You can substitute doctors, hospitals, and patients into the equation, or whichever groups you like: the message is the same.

Users want to explain their requirements in their own language, using their own situation as the context. They want their developers to understand what the problem is, and produce a solution which works their way. The box below gives a short story about staff and customers, with the names changed. You may like to consider whether your organization works the way the system designers in the story did before, or after, that meeting with their customers. A spirit of co-operation is essential.

> **Mary is the marketing manager** in a large multinational. She has found that to be competitive, the customers want the product 25 percent smaller, 40 percent lighter, and a brighter color. The system designers think these are needless constraints and that anything to do with the color is beneath their dignity.
>
> To improve the situation, Mary invites the project manager and a couple of the system designers to come and meet some users. She shows them the latest product, tells them that they can ask any questions of the design team, and asks them for their reaction.
>
> A month later, the product is 25 percent smaller and more brightly colored, and plans are in hand for making it lighter.

Allocate enough effort and resources for requirements

You need access to the best people with the right background for each part of the job. This may mean getting one experienced person from each group of stakeholders for a few weeks or months.

Time to work out a good structure

Getting the requirements structured correctly takes time because the structure depends on what kinds of user there are, on what each kind of user needs the system to do, and on the nature of the constraints. For instance, a safety-critical system has tighter constraints than an office system.

Allow time for gathering, organizing, and checking out the requirements both formally and informally. This isn't something that can be rushed.

Expected effort

To put some numbers to all this, expect to spend about 5 percent of project effort on the requirements, not including system specification or design. Allow a generous chunk of the schedule – up to 25 percent of calendar time – for the requirements on shorter projects, but not more than three months on larger ones. Again, this does not include system specification, which typically takes about 20–25 percent of the time available to the project. If you are taking longer, chances are you are getting into specifying and designing the solution instead of finding out what the users want. Or, different groups of stakeholders are failing to agree on the scope and direction of the project.

Later on, the stakeholders involved in managing the project will naturally revisit the requirements. They will have a great deal of work to do keeping track of progress, drawing missed requirements to the developers' attention, agreeing changes, and ensuring thorough testing. They will use requirements throughout the project, for example, in cost-benefit analysis, in integration, and in change management. You can't freeze the requirements for the life of the project.

Expected time taken

The effort spent on requirements is small in absolute terms, but larger in calendar time, because the requirements team needs fewer people than a design team. These requirements engineers have to be skillful in helping users to express their requirements clearly.

Only the stakeholders can tell you that their requirements are correct, and they may not be used to checking written requirements. You should allow time and effort to devise suitable presentations, animations, models, and prototypes to make the requirements clear.

Prepare for change

Allow for feedback

Whatever you do, make sure you allocate enough time for users to respond. You will never get the whole picture down perfectly at the first attempt. Once you have set up a framework in which users feel comfortable making informal comments on their requirements, you should find it easy and quick to get their agreement on any particular subject. Take time and effort to discuss needs in a relaxed and open way with your users.

Requirements effort throughout the life cycle

Some effort on requirements is needed throughout the project, because compromise and change are inevitable. However much effort you put into them, requirements are inevitably changed through the course of a project. As it becomes clear what is feasible and how much the requirements will cost, you will have to compromise. An essential element in any acceptable compromise is knowing how important each requirement is to its owner. Prioritization and scope are described in Section 6.3.

Allow for change

Changes from outside are also inevitable. Every project with a lifetime of more than a few months will experience pressures from competitors, market or operational changes, from new technologies, and from stakeholders to change the requirements and the design. Organize the requirements so that you can cope with changes, and allow for effort to update the requirements throughout the project.

By the way, expecting change is not an excuse for not doing the requirements well. The more you find out about what the users want early on, the less needless change there will be in the requirements, and the less the project will cost. The cost of making a change to fix a mistake in the requirements rises steeply through a project, so early action pays for itself many times over.

Allow for users' feelings

Some users may be defensive about giving their opinions, especially if, for instance, they think their jobs may be affected by the system being developed. In that situation, it is essential to gain their trust before trying to start developing a system. The only fair way to do this is to make sure that management, users, and developers share an understanding of what the system will mean for the workforce. You need to consider who will really benefit from the use of a system – these are the real stakeholders. Systems are not built solely for the benefit of their operators.

1.6 The requirements writing process

Requirements writing forms a smaller cycle within the larger wheels of system development (Figure 1.1). For all that, it is critical because everything else depends on it. A complete cycle consists of all the steps, from identifying a problem to generating a deliverable product – an agreed set of requirements. It involves close collaboration between stakeholders and requirements engineers.

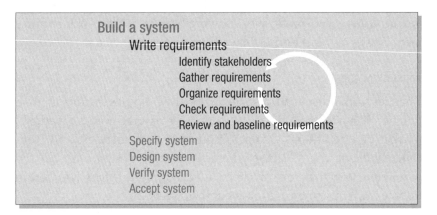

Build a system
Write requirements
Identify stakeholders
Gather requirements
Organize requirements
Check requirements
Review and baseline requirements
Specify system
Design system
Verify system
Accept system

FIGURE 1.1 ■ The requirements writing process within the system life cycle

You will never identify all the stakeholders at the first attempt, nor gather all the requirements. As you check your progress with stakeholders, especially the users, you will inevitably detect more situations that need to be covered by new requirements. You will then repeat the requirements cycle in the light of the newly discovered requirements.

Identify the stakeholders

Most projects start from a single point – a decision made in a meeting, or an enthusiastic advocate of an approach. That gives you a starting point: the person or people to talk to first. They can name other roles involved in the system. Get them to put names to those roles. Arrange to meet those people, and repeat the identification process until you have a complete list of stakeholders. Chapter 2 describes what to do in more detail.

Gather the requirements

Once you have an accurate list of stakeholders, you can plan your approach for gathering the requirements. You can use interviews (Section 3.2), workshops (Section 3.3), prototypes (Section 3.7), or other techniques for working directly with users (Chapter 3). Or you can scan documentary sources to locate possible requirements, and then work with tools and the materials you have gathered to prompt and encourage stakeholders to state their needs (Chapter 4). These techniques are complementary, and many projects benefit from a mixture of approaches.

Organize the requirements

Requirements as gathered are invariably incomplete. They are in various stages of preparation; they contain mistakes, design choices, and ambiguities. Decisions need to be made; context and organization need to be provided. Chapter 5 explains how to begin, by structuring the requirements into a hierarchy which can be read as a family of scenarios.

For example, Figure 1.1 shows the system life cycle as a sequence of very large steps, from writing the requirements to accepting the system. This can be read as a top-level scenario (ending with "… and then the users accept the system"). Each of these steps can be analyzed further. For example, the first step in writing requirements is to identify the stakeholders, but this is itself a process involving smaller steps such as holding interviews and workshops (Chapter 3).

It is easy to assume that the steps form a strict sequence, but this is rarely true in requirements engineering or elsewhere. Instead, there are steps that can be broken down into sets of alternatives, activities that can be carried out in parallel, or which happen only in exceptional circumstances. Once a business process is described in detail, the requirements on each of the smallest steps are simple to write because their purpose is known already.

Chapter 6 explains how to set the requirements into their project context by adding supporting information such as status and traces to other documents. There may also be many relationships between requirements, as when a constraint modifies a desired function.

Chapter 7 discusses requirements writing: something that is simple but not easy, if all the pitfalls of writing vague, confusing, ambiguous, and unverifiable wishes are to be avoided. Good requirements can be written only when a good structure is waiting for them. The essence of good writing is simplicity, and the key to that is to allow each requirement to say just one thing. Requirements become contorted when they are trying to define a behavior, and a performance, and a special case or two, and an alternative behavior all at once. Given a structure that already takes care of all these situations, each requirement can safely ask for just one result.

Check the requirements

Formal reviews are immensely important in improving the quality of requirements, but they are time-consuming. Luckily, informal meetings and discussions can get much of the checking done before a review. The more closely you can work with users, the better. The ideal way to go into a review is knowing that at least the structure of the information is essentially correct. Checking is discussed in Section 8.2.

Review and baseline the requirements

A formal review ensures that everyone gets a final chance to look carefully at their requirements before development starts. A version is circulated, change requests are submitted and sorted, and a meeting decides which changes to accept. The final version is prepared and frozen so that development can go ahead on a known and agreed basis. This is a serious and costly process, justified by its proven effectiveness in fixing problems. Reviewing is described in Section 8.3.

2

Identifying the stakeholders

The first step in gathering requirements is seemingly so obvious that people often ignore it – and miss important sources of requirements. It is to identify who is or should be involved. People often think that they know who will have an interest in a project, but the task of identifying the stakeholders is not as simple as it may look. This chapter illustrates what the challenge consists of, and suggests some simple techniques.

2.1 Different types of stakeholder

It is essential to define the different types of stakeholder. Each type has its own set of requirements, so what you hear depends on who you ask. A complete problem description must represent all relevant viewpoints. Pay special attention to any potential conflicts between viewpoints: it is much better to identify and resolve these before development begins than to find out about incompatibilities during testing or early use.

Example: stakeholders in a space telescope project

Each type of stakeholder wants the results that a future system can deliver to them. Think of the different users of the Hubble Space

Telescope. Then think of who else has an interest in the mission (Figure 2.1).

FIGURE 2.1 ■ Stakeholders in a space telescope project, illustration by Beccy Blake

Astronomers' needs shape the telescope. They want the information that the telescope can collect so that they can solve problems in astrophysics and publish scientific papers. They could ask to point the telescope anywhere in the heavens within 15 minutes – a function with a performance constraint; or for it to be usable for at least ten years – a lifetime availability constraint.

Ground station engineers controlling the telescope want to know that it is working properly, and that the astronomers are getting their information. If their needs are not met, the system will be useless to the astronomers.

Astronauts launching or maintaining the telescope want it to be safe and quick to exchange components on a spacewalk.

The **organization's managers** have objectives for the telescope project so that the telescope and the space agency are seen to be successful. For example, the organization needs competitive products, compatibility with its existing products, and a good return on investment. Management should have no special rights over user requirements, but can influence them indirectly from this business perspective. In commercial companies, product managers typically introduce such requirements.

Politicians are responsible for obtaining funding for the project. They want it to be successful, both for prestige and to guarantee work for the people whose livelihoods depend on the project. Without political support, the project will never be completed.

Each of these groups holds a different stake in requirements territory, but some requirements such as the organization's objectives drive the rest. The requirements have to take account of all these distinct points of view. The requirements ask for results, such as:

"The satellite controller shall be able to point the telescope at a newly discovered object without planning."

Stakeholders often also ask for their requirements to be delivered in a certain way, for example, for the controls to be available all the time; for safety; for performance. For example, the organization may ask:

"The system shall last for nine years."

The users may request that during this operational lifetime:

"Astronomers shall be provided with images with an availability of more than 99 percent each month."

This could flow into several subsystem specifications, such as:

"The image transmission subsystem shall continue to function correctly in the presence of any single component failure."

2.2   Your house extension: a simple case?

The simplest case in identifying the stakeholders is perhaps where you are writing your own requirements, and you are the only user. For example, you may be building a study in an extension to your house.

What could be easier? You are owner, client, author of the requirements, and the sole person you have to please – or are you?

a The local government may have something to say: the planning
department may only allow building in a certain style, up to a
certain height, or up to a maximum volume.

b The building department may want you to comply with building
regulations concerning structural strength, sound and thermal
insulation, electrical safety, fire escapes and more.

c The neighbors have rights too – to light, and to safe use of shared
walls, for instance.

d And what about the other people who live in your house – your
partner, your children? What do they need now, and in a few years'
time?

This simple-looking case perhaps does not look quite so simple any
more. Be warned, identifying the stakeholders in an industrial project
may take some time and effort. But making that effort is much better
and more cost-effective than not identifying them.

2.3 A practical approach to identifying stakeholders

Identify and follow leads

If you have to identify the stakeholders in a company, the first step is
to arrange to meet the client or primary contact. Ask them which
groups of people they believe have a stake in the requirements. For
example, who are their clients and suppliers? If you are with a small
group of stakeholders, a few minutes of brainstorming may enable you
to capture an accurate preliminary list of people who should be
involved.

With management support, which you will certainly need, ask for a
suitable representative of each group, and arrange to meet them. Ask
them the same questions. Repeat the process until you get a stable list
of groups, each represented by at least one suitable contact person.

EXERCISE 1

Listing the stakeholders

Users can be expected to understand their own requirements well. You need to talk to them to find out what they want. But who will you talk to? You need to find out what kinds of stakeholder there are, and who could represent each group. This exercise helps you define the different types of stakeholder. If you are currently starting a project, use it as the example for this exercise.

1   Make a list of the most obvious core types of stakeholder in your project.

2   List the names and job titles of the best people to speak to in each stakeholder group.

If you don't have a suitable project, imagine you are working on a truckers' mobile communications project, where truckers receive messages over a radio network to deliver cargo orders to customers. We have started to fill in the types of stakeholder, with names and job titles, for you.

a   *Truck driver, …*

b   *Jack Schmidt – senior driver; Bill Higgins – assistant driver, …*

3   If you have a real project for this exercise, go and talk to the people you have listed. Ask them who they have to deal with – for instance, clients and suppliers – to achieve their goals. Exclude people seen not to be relevant to the project from your list of stakeholders.

4   Repeat steps (1) through (3) for each of the relevant people named, until the list of stakeholders stabilizes.

Identify the key roles and interactions between them

Once you have a good idea of who the main stakeholders are, it is time to hold an initial workshop. The aim is to identify the basic interactions between actors in the drama. This sharpens up the outlines of the problem, enabling the stakeholders to decide whether each part of the problem should be included within the scope of a future development. Note that not all stakeholders are necessarily involved directly as actors.

It is possible to apply any of a range of more or less formal techniques for this purpose. Aim to ensure that you have buy-in from all the stakeholders, and that you get a simple, agreed description of the part each actor plays. You do not want to get into designing the system at this stage.

If you find you have to refer to a system that the stakeholders want, treat it as a black box. Similarly, if the stakeholders refer to any external system, person, or organization over which they have no control, treat that as an external agent. Both black-box systems and external agents can be involved in interactions as if they were actors. It is often a design issue whether a particular interaction is handled automatically or manually, so that decision can safely be postponed at this stage. You are interested only in finding out the shape of the problem, not in how that problem will one day be solved.

To enable the stakeholders to see what is happening, a diagram is helpful. In the workshop, this need not be neat and tidy, but should be readily understood. Hand-drawn diagrams, in immediate response to what a stakeholder says, are more likely to get everyone involved than formal diagrams prepared after the workshop. We recommend a large whiteboard and colored marker pens so you can quickly draw and revise the diagram as the stakeholders make their contributions. If you have a wall-sized flat screen which you can draw on with a stylus, or a bright data projector and a suitable drawing tool, you may be able to achieve a similar effect electronically.

Figure 2.2 illustrates the case of an ambulance service. This simple notation identifies clearly but not too formally the actors, systems, external agents, and interactions between them. Drawing the diagram is an opportunity to go around the room asking each stakeholder to introduce themselves, state their role – which you immediately write on the board – and say who or what they interact with.

The workshop has already identified three actors and several interactions between them. The use of the incident database has not yet been worked out, but as it is clear to the stakeholders that some such system will certainly be needed, it is shown as a black box.

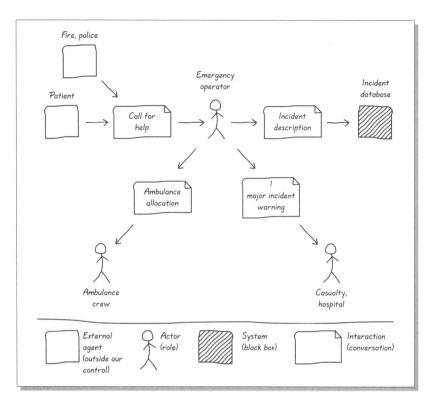

FIGURE 2.2 ■ Diagramming user interactions

The patient, like the fire and police services, is able to interact with the emergency operator, but has no direct access to the ambulance service's information, which is confidential. Therefore patient, fire, and police are external agents rather than actors. The arrows on either side of each interaction indicate the agent who initiated the interaction, and the recipient. Every interaction must be started by one agent, and must involve another agent.

A diagram of user interactions is a model of the context of a future system. It does not define the functions of that system, nor does it say anything about the ways that the system may be used or the order in which interactions may take place. You should take care to avoid putting in too much detail. If stakeholders suggest requirements or design details, write these down and save them for later.

Notice that you are not trying to analyze all possible information flows: this is not a dataflow method. (Agents and their interactions make good candidates for objects in object-oriented analysis and design, but that is outside the scope of this book.) Each message represents a whole interaction, a conversation between agents – not necessarily human. For example, during a call for help from the fire service, the emergency operator may need to ask the identity of the caller and their fire station, and perhaps for authentication. This may involve a whole list of speech acts or information transfers, but only one interaction – with a single direction from initiator to recipient – is shown on the diagram. The ability to receive emergency calls from the fire service may be a crucial requirement, but the requirements too are a matter for later investigation and agreement with the stakeholders.

If you have been taught that requirements must be completed before design may begin, you may wonder why design elements such as the incident database are allowed at this early stage. It is certainly best to understand the problem before trying to solve it, but it is also important to stay in the real world. If the ambulance service has come to you to help them specify their new incident-handling infrastructure, they may already know they need a database. The best the requirements engineer can do is to accept the situation, draw a black box on the diagram, and encourage the stakeholders to put off detailed design decisions until these need to be made.

3

Gathering requirements from stakeholders

Once you have an agreed list of stakeholders, you need to assess the nature and scale of the requirements-gathering task. Then you need to select appropriate techniques for gathering the requirements from the sources you have identified.

In this chapter, we focus on how to get requirements directly from stakeholders, whether through interviews or workshops. In the next chapter, we examine a wide range of other possible sources of requirements, and consider some of the pitfalls in extracting requirements from documents.

3.1 Possible techniques

Ultimately, requirements express human needs. A business finds that its customers and internal users start to

- send in problem reports about an existing product;
- complain about how difficult and slow some process is; or
- change a device or a piece of software to work the way they want.

Users may not be able to imagine a new system or how they would use it, but they know what their problem is, and why they would like it fixed. They are the experts in their own problem. You need a range of techniques to get the requirements for their project.

Techniques for capturing requirements include interviewing users and other stakeholders, holding workshops, observing users at work, searching likely documents, and seeing the changes that users have made to existing systems. Problem reports and suggestions from existing systems can be valuable sources of requirements, provided you find out and record how important each proposed requirement is to its users. New technologies suggest opportunities rather than requirements as such, but the pressure of competition can quickly turn a possible new approach into a definite business requirement – when the technologies appear in rival products, for instance.

Sources of requirements

Interviews

Workshops

Experiencing life as a user

Observing users at work

Acting out what needs to happen

Prototypes

Problem reports

Helpdesk and support team

Trainers and consultants

Customer suggestions and complaints

Improvements made by users

Unintended uses of products

Comparable and rival products

Existing designs and specifications

Badly written contracts

In typical engineering developments, the engineer is personally responsible for the product design, whether for a bridge, a circuit, or a computer program. Requirements are different. Your job is to see that the requirements are captured correctly, are organized properly, are complete, and are well expressed – you may even write them. But the requirements themselves don't belong to you.

The core of the process is to get the requirements down quickly, and then to encourage the stakeholders to correct and improve them. Your part is to put in those corrections at once, and to repeat the cycle. You should start with the best structure you can devise, but expect to keep on correcting it throughout the process.

You can sometimes capture requirements from existing documents, especially if someone has already studied the problem, but stakeholders must remain the primary source. Especially if you do the writing, you need to make sure that the stakeholders feel that they own the requirements. Expect a period of intense interaction with stakeholders, whether in individual interviews or in group workshops.

Clients may ask whether they should send out questionnaires to their staff to help you gather requirements. This is a rather passive technique which rarely works well, as forms sent out to non-stakeholders dilute the response, and pre-printed questions often fail to find out what people really need. If you already knew what the problem was, why would you be asking users at all? To succeed, requirements gathering has to be much more interactive, and must focus on people's needs. This means meeting people and encouraging them to speak: no questionnaire can do that.

The power of why

Asking "why" questions is a powerful way of searching out user requirements, whether you ask yourself, get groups of users to discuss the question, or directly interview a single user or other stakeholder.

You can tell when you have found the root of a user requirement, as you will reach something simple like "because that's what I want." The question "why?" used by itself can seem quite threatening, so take care. "Why" questions can be formulated unaggressively in many ways, such as:

- What is the purpose of that?
- Can you explain why you need it to do that?
- What was the thinking behind that?
- What is the underlying reason for that?

For example, if a user says

"The coffeepot must be made of stainless steel."

you could ask why they need that particular material. The immediate answer might be

"Because a glass pot might break."

Why should it break?

"Because the pot is often left on the heat even when empty."

How does that happen? Can you explain why it matters?

"Because the pot is shared by many people who just pass through, and the heater does not switch off when the pot is empty."

Why doesn't it switch off?

"Because … a requirement was missed."

Therefore we can write down an improved requirement – one of several:

The coffeepot heater should switch off when the pot is empty.

This is better but is still more like a system specification than a user requirement. *Why* do we mind if the pot breaks? Because it costs money, does material damage, and could cause injury. Therefore the user requirements might be:

I want hot fresh coffee whenever I walk into the kitchen.

I want to be able to make coffee without risking injury or damage.

Asking "why?"

1   Try to improve on the coffeepot requirements discussed above.

2   Devise suitable "why…" questions for the following situation, see where they lead, and draft user requirements for the underlying problem:

Existing design: The bottle-warmer displays a red light when the power is applied, but the light goes out when the specified temperature is reached.

Hint: separate out the requirements from the design solution. Was the implied design good? What might have driven it?

Users are the primary source of requirements. Unless you are a user yourself, and perhaps even if you are, you will need to make an effort to understand and experience the users' problem to describe it successfully.

There are four major ways of doing this:

- interviews;
- workshops;
- experiencing life as a user;
- studying existing documents (see Chapter 4).

These approaches are described in turn below and in Chapter 4.

3.2 Interviews

Interviews can be an excellent source of requirements, provided users are given room to speak. You need to decide in advance how much structure you will provide, and what style of interviewing you will use.

Structured interviewing with a script of questions to ask is sometimes helpful for checking specific points, but it prevents the sort of free discussion which often brings new requirements into the open. The old kind of "structured interview" tended to limit what the user could say to what the developers thought would be important. More open styles of interviewing are described below.

Open discussions can be held in one-to-one or small group interviews, or in workshops involving larger numbers of users. Techniques for holding effective interviews and workshops are discussed below.

Face-to-face contact with users through individual interviewing is an important way to gather and validate requirements, but remember that it is not the only possible technique, and that interviews can be run in many different styles. What suits one kind of problem and one organization may not work on another. Ask your colleagues how they prepare for interviews and what kinds of questions they ask. If you have the opportunity, accompany an experienced colleague and watch what they do. Develop a repertoire of styles to suit different situations.

Plan your interviews

Before planning interviews or workshops, find out what kinds of users there are, and who it would be best to speak to in each group (as described in Chapter 2). To do this, you may need two or three planning meetings with user representatives or their management.

The first meeting tends to be formal: management present their organization, their project, and perhaps a little on the problem they would like to solve; you present your general approach. This helps everyone to get to know each other, and gives you a feel for the organization and context.

At the next planning meeting, discuss what you would like to achieve, and why: a clear set of user requirements to define the problem in detail. After that, you can work with the user representatives or managers to identify and arrange interviews with suitable users. Other kinds of meeting, such as workshops, demonstrations, and factory tours, should also be considered.

Interviews work best when you have a clear structure in your mind:

■ introductions;

■ explanation of your mission;

■ time for the interviewee to describe the problem;

■ questions you might ask;

■ materials you might use.

You do not have to show this structure to interviewees. You will probably find you move away from it, on to areas that they want to tell you about, but a plan is still worth making as it gives you a way to get started and a source of ideas in case an interviewee does not say much.

Structured or unstructured?

We suggest that you plan interviews in some detail but appear relaxed to users so that they can speak freely. Start by setting the scene. Their organization is thinking of addressing problem such-and-such by funding a study of the problem area, having a set of requirements written, and then probably having a system built to meet the need. The problem involves various kinds of users, and the interviewee fits into the picture here and here.

Explain your current understanding of who does what, maybe by pointing to a simple diagram or sketch, such as an interaction diagram (Figure 3.1; see Section 2.3 for details). It may help if you draw the diagram in front of the interviewee, as this shows that your view is not fixed and allows them to intervene. You can then encourage the interviewee to say whether your understanding is right, and if not, in which way it could be improved. After that, you can get them to describe what they know and do, and to point out any difficulties they have experienced using the current system.

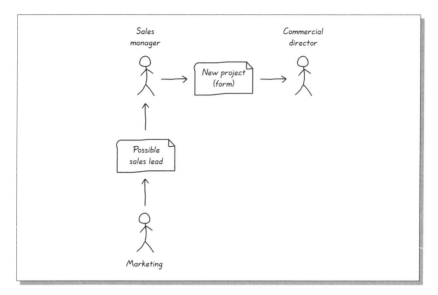

FIGURE 3.1 ■ Using a rough sketch to encourage interviewees

Record what is said – note-taking, audio, and video

Our experience is that interviewing is best approached as a two-person job. The first person stimulates the users and synthesizes their answers, while the second person, the writer, further refines that information, asking for clarification when necessary. Within minutes of the interview, you can deliver a copy of the notes to users for correction or expansion.

Even the best note-takers can miss subtle points, especially if the interviewee uses ordinary-sounding words as technical terms. For example, in computing, words like "table," "record," and "word" have precise meanings. Other professions do the same with other words. Therefore, we recommend that you record your interviews.

Ask the interviewee's permission to make a recording. Some people find it alarming or distracting to see a tape recorder, and in some areas there may be confidentiality concerns. Assure stakeholders that you will keep sensitive information confidential, and take care to do so. Remember that you may need special permission to record in some organizations. A pocket-sized tape recorder is ideal for taping interviews.

Analyzing recordings is labor-intensive, and causes a delay before getting the information back to interviewees for correction. If you rely on getting a transcript of the tape, you delay the process of synthesizing the results and enabling the interviewees to respond. Instead, use the tape just to fill in gaps where you feel you may have missed something. Rapid feedback to stakeholders makes them feel involved in the process as they are able to correct the draft requirements quickly.

Video could be useful for capturing images which explain what words cannot – how a process looks in a factory, for example. But video requires an enormous amount of analysis, causes even longer delays than audio, and in any case does not substitute for well-written requirements.

It is worth making a rough draft for immediate review by the interviewee. You can improve the text later, but nothing equals the power of getting the interviewee to own his or her requirements there and then.

Use open, not leading, questions

The key skill in interviewing is to get stakeholders talking, so they start telling you what they need rather than what they think you want to hear. Ways not to do this include asking leading questions which imply what sort of answer you expect, and talking so much that interviewees hardly get to say anything.

Open questioning is more likely to be effective, especially at the start of interviews. For instance, if you have a diagram based on previous interviews, you can explain what the diagram says, and then ask:

"Is that an accurate description of how you see it?" or

"Can you improve on this description?" or simply

"How would you describe this?"

Or, ask specifically what you want to know, but in an open-ended way:

"What are the biggest problems you face when doing this task?"

Many people have a tendency to agree with suggestions put to them, so avoid giving your view of a problem. Instead you could say, *"One person suggested that this problem might have that particular cause. What do you think?"* or more generally, *"What do you feel is the main cause of this problem?"* This type of question gives the user permission to express an opinion, even if they are not sure it is correct.

Use sketches and diagrams to clarify requirements

Users will sometimes explain business processes to you with sketches or diagrams, or may have agreed diagrams already available. These represent the way users understand their problem, which often has an existing system as a major element. Ask for copies of any such diagrams, and as long as they make the document more understandable, put them in the requirements.

For example, a sailboat designer may have a preliminary concept for making the product quick to put away and compact to tow behind a family car (Figure 3.2). Take care to state whether each diagram represents a definite requirement or is just an example. The stakeholders may want to illustrate their concept but still leave freedom for systems design. In the case of this sailboat, the design is just an idea, but the ability to tow the boat is a requirement.

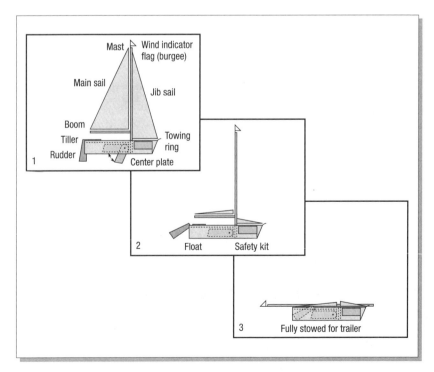

FIGURE 3.2 ■ Sequence of informal diagrams illustrating a requirement

At other times, you may be trying to understand how a system works at present. Sketches can often convey what you understand better than words, and allow users to correct you more easily.

Complete sets of formal diagrams, as used in software and systems engineering, are not really suitable for user requirements. Even if users can understand the notation, they are unlikely to take the time to check through more than one or two diagrams. There is evidence that people who are not systems engineers read all diagrams – state transitions, dataflows, object hierarchies, agent interactions, whatever – as if they were flowcharts, so don't expect too much from formal diagrams as far as users are concerned.

Perhaps the greatest danger here is that people tend to accept any confident-looking set of diagrams as correct, rather than asking themselves whether a picture actually makes sense, or is complete and consistent. The worst answer a user can give you is, "Oh, that looks okay." This answer means that their eyes have glazed over and they will not notice any mistakes. Make sure you encourage and get real comments from involved users.

Use models from earlier interviews

After a few interviews, you will start to develop an understanding of the problem. Define it in a draft document and get interviewees to correct it. A simple diagram (no more elaborate than Figure 3.1) that describes how you think a process may work can be useful. You can say:

"It looks as if this is happening, and then that. Are these steps right? Have I missed anything out?"

The interviewees can then correct you. Soon they start describing their own area in detail, and you can pick out requirements from what they say. The draft requirements form the basis for discussing what stakeholders actually want in subsequent interviews.

Use documents, hardware parts, photographs

Visual aids that can be effective in eliciting requirements include:

- the description of a process in an organization's quality manual;
- a hardware part – ask users to explain how it is made, and what part they played in its design;
- a photograph of a system or process;
- mock-ups of computer screens.

These help to trigger stakeholders into talking about what they want. You are aiming to find what users and other stakeholders actually need: if this is not like the object you have presented, that is fine, as you have stimulated them to express their requirements. Stakeholders may never have seen their needs expressed in this way, or so clearly, so give them the time to say what they feel in their own style.

Check your interpretations with the users

It is helpful to approach a series of interviews with the intention of discovering what the stakeholders actually want, and then checking back with them that your interpretation of what was said is correct. You can start the ball rolling during the interview itself by feeding back to the interviewees what you think they said:

"So if I've understood this, you start by…"

They will soon tell you if your ideas aren't right.

Once you have written up the interview as a set of requirements or interview notes, you must get your account checked out by the interviewees. Even if you wrote down what was said verbatim, there may still be errors and omissions in the account. This is to your advantage: you are finding out things that were missed in the interview. Users are human and fallible, and need space to make mistakes so as to explain themselves fully.

Don't expect to get everything done in one interview. The minimum is one face-to-face meeting, and one exchange of documents. Key users should be interviewed more than once.

Show users how they will benefit

Interviews work only if users see that what is being done is important and will not harm them. As soon as they understand that their requirements will actually drive the development, they will want to ensure you understand their needs accurately. Provided they see the task as serious, you will have their full co-operation.

3.3 Workshops

A workshop requires more preparation and is a larger occasion than an interview, but it is inherently more interactive and offers an unparalleled opportunity for stakeholders to propose, evaluate, and agree their requirements.

Advantages

A workshop approach rapidly puts together a good set of requirements (Figure 3.3). In 2–5 days, a group of stakeholders facilitated by a pair of requirements engineers can create a workable set of requirements. The process is a cycle, in which everyone is free to suggest improvements. For example, when all workshop participants try to estimate the cost and value of each requirement, the requirements steadily become more practical.

Workshops are quicker and better at discovering requirements than other techniques such as sending out questionnaires. They bring the right collection of people together, and enable them to correct and improve on their own requirements.

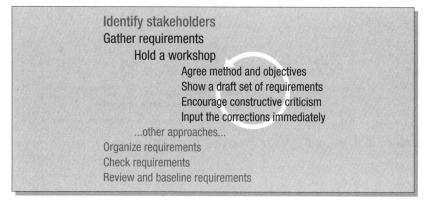

FIGURE 3.3 ■ Logic of the requirements workshop

Costs and benefits

A workshop is expensive because of the number of people involved but should more than pay for itself. For example, if you can define a product correctly the first time around, and cut three months off the requirements phase, the savings will be enormous.

Workshop room layout

The workshop space has to be carefully organized to encourage free and open dialog involving all the participants (Figure 3.4). The room layout for a workshop is important, as every item has a job to do. Information has to be recorded smoothly and efficiently, and everybody must feel involved in the process as an equal partner.

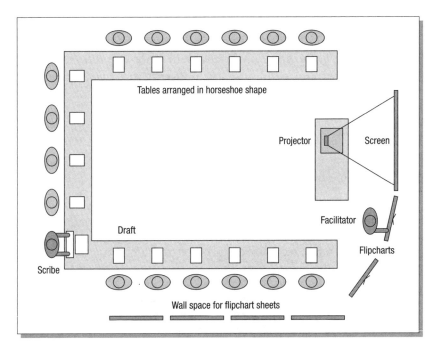

FIGURE 3.4 ■ The room layout for a workshop is important

Planning a workshop

The workshop must be planned in detail to make the best use of people's time. Here are some practical tips:

- Choose a quiet location, so that people are not disturbed by day-to-day business. If the stakeholders are very busy, consider a weekend workshop in an attractive location.

- Prevent interruptions by allowing no mobile phones; instead, arrange to take messages externally.

- Encourage informal interactions by choosing a site so that people do not go home at night or go out separately.

- Order refreshments and light meals to get people talking amongst themselves without feeling they have to express perfect requirements immediately.

Ensure that the workshop location has facilities for printing and photo-copying complete sets of draft documents, quickly. Hotels in particular often claim impressive facilities, but in practice the lone receptionist may have no time for more than a couple of sheets, delivered several hours too late. This alone can be fatal to a workshop, so try the "could you make me 12 copies of this by 2PM" test in advance. Make sure the location management understand that this is critical if they want your business.

A co-operative approach

The role of the workshop is to bring stakeholders together for a common purpose, which is to create an agreed draft of the user requirements. The workshop is most likely to be effective if participants understand what is wanted from them. They can prepare for the workshop by identifying and bringing along any relevant reference materials. It may help if you begin with a short period of training in whichever co-operative approach you favor. That knowledge can then immediately be applied to the stakeholders' project.

An approach for workshops on any subject, not just to gather requirements, has been pioneered by John Heron over many years. In his book, *Co-operative Inquiry* (Sage, 1996), he describes a simple inquiry cycle technique (Figure 3.5).

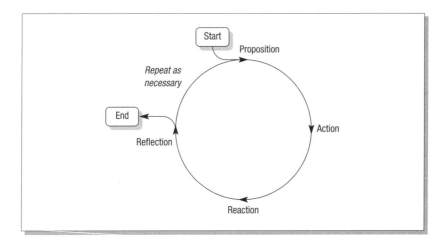

FIGURE 3.5 ■ Inquiry cycle for a workshop

In this approach, a workshop begins when someone proposes a course of action, such as that the stakeholders should each say what their role is. That action follows if everyone agrees. An action can involve all workshop participants, or can be delegated to an individual or to a subgroup. Things may have been said that not everyone agrees with or that provoke new ideas, such as additional requirements. The workshop therefore allows time for the stakeholders to react to what has been said. When any tensions have been resolved, the workshop reflects on whether the action seems to be complete, or whether another round is needed. This is quite a general method which has proven its effectiveness in different fields. When requirements are being gathered, tensions such as conflicts between different viewpoints can be strong. Co-operative inquiry is a known way of resolving these.

Colin Potts has independently developed an inquiry cycle method called SCENiC specifically for requirements. His cycle takes a document, allows the inquiry to challenge it, and conducts a reasoned discussion involving questions, answers, and reasons, which are documented, leading to a decision on how to evolve the requirements. The method involves analyzing scenarios (see Chapter 5) to help stakeholders and researchers gain insight into the requirements. This leads to a change to the requirements document, where the cycle repeats.

Whether or not you choose a particular method for your workshop approach, your workshops will probably require a pair of requirements engineers working together to facilitate the process and to document the requirements. They are labeled as 'facilitator' and 'scribe' in Figure 3.4.

Starting the workshop

On the first morning of a workhop you could start off, for example, by:

- getting the participants to define the different types of users for the system;
- teaching about the organization of user requirements;
- getting the participants to define a good structure for requirements;
- letting the participants define the responsibilities for the structure;
- splitting up the group into the separate user interests, and starting to fill in the structure;
- teaching the group about reviewing;
- letting each group present their work for review by other participants;
- updating the material with the review decisions.

The harder the group works, the better, so dividing into small groups that work concurrently can be advantageous. Groups need to report their findings to ensure the whole workshop agrees.

Redrafting the requirements – in the workshop

Now you have a rough draft of a set of requirements – the perfect starting point for improvement. While the stakeholders take a break for lunch, go through the requirements quickly and clean them up. When the workshop restarts, the first version is waiting for the stakeholders. They will certainly not agree with what it says. Let them cover draft versions in red ink, and input the sensible comments. Repeat the process until exhaustion sets in, and take everyone out for a good meal.

During the workshop you need not be at all formal about the change control process – that is necessary only when the requirements reach a reasonable level of quality. But you must make sure that you know where every change comes from, and collect all the notes and forms from the informal review.

Clean up the requirements – after the workshop

Plan for a clean-up after the workshop. Inevitably, after such a frenzied experience the requirements will be untidy, and you will have made mistakes.

Take time to:

- go through the inputs carefully,
- clean up the requirements;
- send out the revised version for further comments; and
- thank the participants for their efforts.

3.4 Experiencing life as a user

A direct way to gather requirements is to experience the user's work for yourself. This is only possible when the work is not too complex or too dangerous to be undertaken by non-experts. If users are involved in electronic engineering, for example, it is possible that one of your colleagues may have a background in that field. That person could be assigned to go and work directly with users for a period – perhaps a month – and then help the users to write the requirements.

Working with users helps you understand problems that have resisted previous solutions. Familiar systems developed in this way include many excellent tools for programmers, such as interactive editors and compilers, as the developers naturally had both the expertise in the subject area and their own interests at heart. It takes more effort to apply the approach to other fields, but the results can justify the investment.

3.5 Observing users at work

Where the work cannot easily be experienced directly, it may still be possible to do better than just sit quietly and watch. There are many documented techniques for gathering requirements by observing.

These may be unfamiliar to many systems engineers, but are well known to human–computer interaction designers.

For example, users can give you a running commentary on what they are doing, what the problems are, and what they would like to have to make the work easier. You can ask for explanations at quieter moments. Tape recording is advisable with this technique. You can consider whether video would help you to understand the problem, or simply overwhelm you with material.

A few photographs may be useful, both for explaining the context to system designers, and for prompting users for requirements later: "What do you need to do in this situation?" A small tape recorder may be the best means of making notes during observation periods, especially if things happen rapidly, as you do not need to look away as you would if writing. If you are planning to use this technique, budget for time to analyze the tape as well as the observation periods.

3.6 Acting out what needs to happen

Where the work involves complex transactions between different users, there may be so much happening that it is difficult for the engineer to understand the situation – air traffic control is an extreme example. Decisions may be made on the basis of different pieces of evidence; parts of a transaction may be conducted simultaneously by different users; different conditions may lead to many alternative paths. You can disentangle the threads by looking at one scenario at a time.

A simple, enjoyable, and effective technique is to gather the users in a mini-workshop, and step through the scenarios they think are important, to identify who does what and when (Figure 3.6). You need some physical tokens, such as small bean-bags like those used to practice juggling. The first role-player takes a token, says out loud their role and what they are doing, and throws the token to the next user. If two or more simultaneous activities follow, the first role-player takes two tokens and passes each to the appropriate role-player. The two tokens are passed on as necessary until a single activity follows on from both of them. When the parallel streams of activities merge, one of the tokens is set aside, and a single token is used from then on.

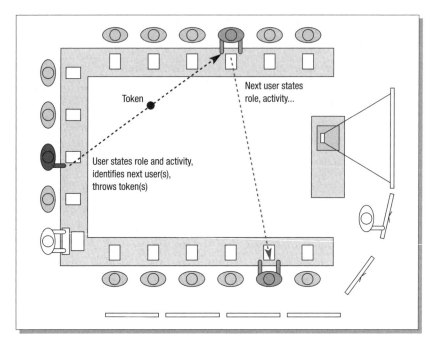

Token

Next user states
role, activity...

User states role and activity,
identifies next user(s),
throws token(s)

FIGURE 3.6 ■ Stepping through a scenario powerfully assists understanding

Users have a clear idea of their own roles, and they know who should give them a token and who they give their tokens to. They may well be surprised, though, by what happens to the tokens before and after their own activities, so expect lively discussions.

Note carefully the following details for each step:

- preconditions (e.g. activities a, b completed);
- role (there should be just one);
- name of user with that role;
- activity;
- product/result of that activity;
- whether there is a choice to be made. (*Users may tell you this, or you may have to ask them later.*)

If as we suggest you have two requirements engineers working together, one can write down these details while the other builds up an agent interaction diagram (see Figure 2.2). Each stakeholder is drawn as an actor with a named role; each activity corresponds to a message, usually from one actor to another. If stakeholders mention external systems, these are drawn on the diagram as external agents.

Some requirements engineers, such as Suzanne Robertson (see Further reading), systematically write out a card like those used in libraries for each step, with the details, the date, the engineer's initials, and so on. This technique makes it easy to rearrange steps if they are out of order, and the cards can be valuable in encouraging interviewees to point out errors and omissions.

This information allows you to build up a clear and accurate account of the different ways a future system would be used, and how they fit together to describe the problem. Ways of using a system are known as scenarios or "use cases." The concept of the use case was introduced by Ivar Jacobson to describe different ways of using a telecommunications system, and then generalized for many other purposes. This is a great start, but when there are many use cases, fitting them together is a serious problem. Alistair Cockburn suggested that problem descriptions need to be organized into one coherent structure representing sequences of users' goals. We would go further and argue that the structure should also identify parallel paths and alternatives. In addition, it must describe how to deal with any exceptions that might prevent users' goals from being reached. Cockburn also added "guarantees," such as that the attempt to reach a goal will not delete any data recorded earlier, preconditions (whatever has to be true before a use case may start), and triggers (the events that cause a use case to begin). These are excellent ideas as they make the users' intentions clearer.

A simple way of structuring the requirements is explained in Chapter 5. Essentially, the idea is to construct a basic heading structure as a list of steps towards a desired goal, and then to analyze each step in more detail as if it was a goal. Any scenarios you capture during interviews or workshops can go straight in as sequences of headings. At the end of this process, each of the lowest-level steps is a small-scale goal that can be satisfied by one or a very few requirements.

3.7 Prototypes

As soon as we see a working model, we know how it could be improved. A simple prototype can provoke users into giving good requirements or into changing their minds about existing requirements. However, make it clear that your prototype just demonstrates some ideas, and is not a finished product or even a decision about the approach – the way you present a prototype is crucial.

The techniques described here are to help you gather ideas for requirements. You need to share these with users to find out whether your ideas match their actual needs. Prototypes and models, handled with care, are an excellent way of presenting ideas to users. They can illustrate how an approach might work, or give users a glimpse of what they might be able to do. Of course, more requirements are likely to emerge when users see what you are suggesting.

A presentation can use a sequence of slides, an artist's impression, or even an animation to give users a vision of the possibilities. The prototype design for a television advertisement or film is a storyboard.

Showing simple mock-ups to improve requirements

You do not necessarily need to create software or equipment for a prototype. A valuable early prototype for an air traffic controller's console was a mock-up made of plywood and printed paper. This prototype was meant to discover whether the control and display layout would be workable. The controls at the back had to be moved because some controllers could not reach them. The prototype had improved the requirements immediately.

Screen mock-ups to capture user interface requirements

When prototyping software, make a mock-up of the user interface "screens," emphasizing that there is no code and the system has not been designed or even specified yet: there are dangers here for the unwary. Effective screens can be made without programming by using a user interface designer's toolkit, a website editor – letting you simulate actions by navigating between pages – or even a presentation tool. It might even be an advantage if the screens do not look too realistic.

Stimulating users to say what they want

Such prototyping aims to get users to express requirements which were missed previously. You are not trying to sell users an idea or product, you are finding out what they actually want. Seeing a prototype, which invariably is "wrong" in some ways and "right" in others, is a powerful stimulus to users to start saying what they want. They may point out numerous problems with the prototype. This is to be welcomed, as each problem leads to a new requirement.

Recording rapid feedback when demonstrating prototypes

Incidentally, users are often particularly fluent with their comments in the few minutes when they first see or interact with a prototype. This flood of information is valuable, but hard to record on paper. For example, it may be clear from the users' reactions whether a screen design is right or wrong. A tape or video recording, or a second requirements engineer who only takes notes, can be useful at this crucial moment.

4

Other sources of requirements

In the previous chapter we described some techniques for gathering requirements directly from stakeholders, principally through interviews and workshops. There are many other possible sources of requirements; in this chapter we consider what these are and how to exploit them. We also look at the special cases of mass-market products, and user requirements within subsystem projects.

4.1 Possible sources

Perhaps the key concept to bear in mind when gathering requirements is that the requirements belong to the users – and sometimes to other stakeholders. Documents and other sources can suggest possible candidate requirements, but only the stakeholders can tell you whether they actually want these things.

Problem reports

Problems reported by users can often be turned around into requirements. Efficient organizations have a form for reporting problems or software bugs. You can ask to look through these reports.

Your first task is to sort the reports into groups to identify the key areas troubling users. You can then ask users some questions about these areas to clarify their actual needs, based on your reading of the problem reports. For example, there may well be something tricky in the user interface if a series of order entry clerks report that the last record they enter is lost but the developers argue that the record-entry function works just fine. Perhaps when you step on to a "New Record," the previous record is saved automatically, but when you press "Exit," you have to know that you should have pressed "Save and Commit all Records" first. The developers may be right that this is perfectly correct, but if the users are confused there is a requirement in there somewhere.

Helpdesk and support team

Product and service organizations have a helpdesk which keeps a log of problems and fixes, and a support team who do the fixing. Many organizations have similar facilities to support their own operations. Talking to the helpdesk staff and the support team may give you good leads into the requirements, and save you time.

If your helpdesk and support team are unused to gathering requirements, they may need encouragement, specific training, or tools to get them collecting requirements regularly. Their jobs make much more sense when the problems they see every day start to turn into opportunities for enhanced products and services.

A simple word-processor template with entries for Author, Date, Problem, Urgency, Suggested Solution, and finally Investigation and Action Taken, can help to turn problems into requirements. If you have a large system, a requirements management tool will pay for itself many times over by helping you to organize problem reports and trace them to requirements.

Trainers and consultants

Take the time to talk to your training team and consultants. They have intense contact with your clients and a clear view of what users find difficult. Prime both groups to collect requirements continuously: this is interesting for them, stresses their value to the organization, and ties them into development. Make sure they hear what happens to their suggestions.

Customer suggestions and complaints

Another good source of requirements is a list of suggestions and complaints made by customers. The best of these are practically requirements, such as when a customer asks why a mass-market product couldn't do something that the customer wanted.

Keep a single central list of suggestions, and track it. You can use it to start discussions with users, for example by asking them which items in the list they think are most important. As with problem reports, sort the suggestions into groups. Each well-defined group points to a problem area. Find out which users know most about each area, and discuss that group of suggestions with them. You should be able to define some requirements directly. Store suggestions that are too far ahead for immediate implementation in a "waiting room" for possible future use.

Improvements made by users

Improvements made to products by their users are an excellent source of requirements. Users of a standard company spreadsheet may have added a few fields, or related different sheets together, or drawn a graph which exactly meets their individual needs. You need only ask "what is that for?" or "why did you add that?" to get to the actual requirement.

This applies equally to hardware and non-computer devices. For example, a lathe operator may have manufactured a special clamp, or an arm that prevents movement of the tool beyond a certain point. Any such modification points to a requirement for the new version.

Unintended uses

Users are immensely creative in the way that they actually use systems. Look out for usage which was never intended. Mr Uzi, a weapon designer, was surprised to see soldiers using the carefully designed foresight of his gun to open bottles of beer. Horrified, Uzi went back to his office and thought about how to keep the foresights in good condition. Built into the stock of every gun, there is now a can and bottle opener.

The same can happen for software. An observant product manager noticed that an engineer was staying in the office late to use an advanced computer-aided design system to design a new kitchen layout for his home. This opened up a market for inexpensive commercial products, with names such as "Kitchen Designer," for home use.

Comparable products

Existing products often contain working versions of good ideas for solving your users' problems. You can avoid "reinventing the wheel" by looking at what is already on the market, whether installed at the users' site or products made by rival organizations. Even if they are trying to solve slightly different problems, they often give valuable clues to what you should be doing.

You can carefully show some such products to users (as with prototypes, Section 3.7), explaining that this idea is from another area but contains an interesting concept: would it help them? However, not all users can make the imaginative jump from one kind of product to another, so this approach has to be handled cautiously.

Old designs and specifications

Extracting user requirements from documents written for other purposes is far from easy. The text may be out of date; it may represent a particular point of view with which other users disagree; or it may use specialized language that users will have to explain to you. In all of these cases, there is a risk that, unless you discuss what you take from the document with users, you will be inventing a requirement that does not exist.

Check out your ideas with users, trying to:

- draft possible requirements;
- correct requirements that seem inconsistent with the documents;
- build up a case for identified needs, for particular resources (such as users with a specific skill), or simply for time and money to get the requirements worked out properly.

There are powerful reasons for looking at user documents. The difficulty, naturally, is that users may have huge amounts of documentation on company standards, procedures, publicity material, and existing products. Ask users to guide you to relevant items. For example, publicity and user manuals tend to stress what works, rather than what doesn't. You need to find out not what the product does but what users feel it ought to do. That means you have to talk to users, not just read the book.

Badly written contracts

The starting point for many projects is an existing document, either a contract or a report written for management. Often these documents were never intended as formal sets of requirements, and are not a suitable basis for development. You may have won a contract based on such a document from your client. Although you know it is poorly organized, you are committed to developing a system against it. The requirements it contains may be full of holes, unrealistic, poorly organized, and repetitive. Nevertheless, they have contractual force.

Moving from a contract to a structured, verifiable set of requirements is both a technical and a human problem. The customer may insist on using the original document, however impractical that is, and regardless of what the users in the customer's organization actually want.

Whatever happens, you have to agree a coherent and practical set of requirements with your customer. You first need to understand the source document, which involves reading it from end to end several times. The next step is to classify the information. The document may contain the following types of information, of variable quality, and all mixed up:

- user requirements;
- system specifications;
- design elements;
- plans;
- background material;
- irrelevant detail.

Mark up the original text to separate out the requirements; then create an information structure, and put the information of each type into the right box. Then you can structure the information in each box properly, and clean up the wording of the requirements.

The next step is to find a good structure for each of the different types of information. You might choose a set of scenarios for the user requirements, an analysis of functions and constraints for the system specifications, and an object-oriented architecture for the design.

At this stage, the responsibility for owning information becomes much more of an issue. Each set of information has an owner – user requirements have to be agreed with the different user groups, the management plan is owned by the project manager, while the system designer owns the architecture. All of these issues were hidden in the original unstructured information, allowing arbitrary decisions to be made without responsibility.

Organizing the information shows up gaps and overlaps. This should help you convince the customer that the original document needs to be reworked. Point out requirements which are necessary but not included in the original document. Show the customer inconsistencies in the original text. It should not be too hard to encourage a thoughtful customer to understand the problems and agree to improve the contract.

EXERCISE 3

Extracting requirements from source documents

The text in the example below is from a customer who considers it a good definition of what is needed.

Specification

a The project is for a database to store information about the historical performance of projects. **(b)** It will enable users to find out what the original schedules were and **(c)** compare them with current projected plans. **(d)** The system will be easy to use by all managers, and **(e)** be accessible from all workstations in the organization. **(f)** The system will be made in Oracle, and **(g)** shall have an acceptable level of performance across the organization.

h   The system will also produce the progress status of all projects on a monthly basis for the CEO.

i   The screen will show trend charts of predicted versus actual dates for achieving milestones, and **(j)** predict the most likely date of completion of the project.

k   The system must be working satisfactorily by December 2002, and **(l)** will be produced by the information systems department, **(m)** under the management of the systems engineering department. **(n)** The software shall run on PCs.

Classify the statements (a) to (n) into the following types:

1   user requirements: _____

2   system specifications: _____

3   design elements: _____

4   plans: _____

5   background material: _____

6   irrelevant detail: _____

Extracting requirements

The second part of the task of getting requirements from documents is simple: you copy out the relevant bits of text, recording precisely where they came from. This task is easiest with a requirements tool such as DOORS (Figure 4.1). It gives you a database-like structure for recording the status of each requirement beside the actual text. In the illustration, each item has in the left-hand column a unique identifier, invaluable for referring to requirements during a review. The requirement text is in the next column, in this case worded traditionally with "shall" statements. The third column has been set up to display the source of each requirement.

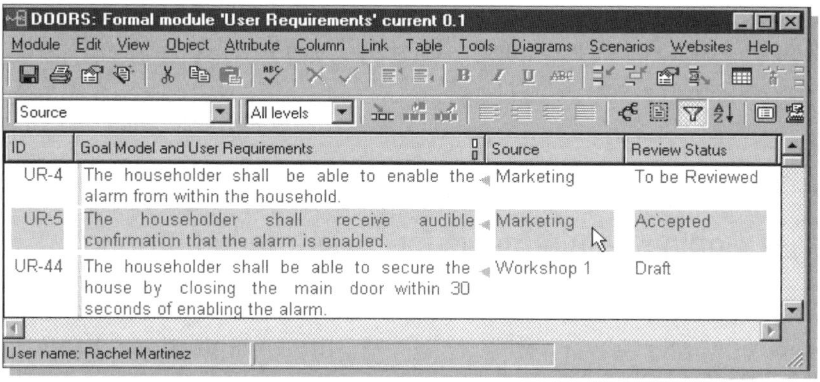

FIGURE 4.1 ■ Requirement text and source recorded in a tool

EXERCISE 4

Extracting requirements from a memo

The marketing director has sent you a memo containing the material for several requirements. Pull out the relevant bits of text, and rephrase them as good individual requirements.

Memo

From : Jane Smith (Marketing Director)

To :   David Kmiec (Product Director)

Re :   Opportunity for small family sailboat

Hi David,

Following my visit to the boat show, I believe I have identified an exciting new opportunity to
extend the company's product range. Our existing products could be supplemented by a
small family sailboat. This would fill an additional market niche, yielding additional revenue
without hurting existing sales.

The sailboat should be attractively packaged to be fun for all the family to sail on lake, river,
or coastal water. It will be safe and easy to handle, whether by the parents or the kids.

Its target price will be set aggressively low to achieve volume sales. It will be sized to fit readily in the home's garage, and will be towed behind a compact family car.

What do you think? I'll get Surveys to find out what styling would be best for next season.

Jane

Project/further work: develop the ideas into a set of user requirements for the sailboat. Include sections for market and safety requirements. You might like to revisit this project when you have read more of this book.

4.2 Getting requirements for mass-market products

Requirements for mass-market products present a special problem: you can't interview a million users. Product organizations therefore have to gather requirements in other ways. The marketing department in particular, which has the job of identifying trends and communicating with users, is ideally placed to serve as a source of user requirements. It can act as a kind of surrogate user.

The vital role of the marketing department

In product organizations, then, the marketing department is the natural home for user requirements. Systems engineers have to rely on the marketing team, who can do surveys, commission prototypes, launch trial products, look at the success of competitors, and monitor market reactions to find out what will sell. Unfortunately, in many firms the relations between systems engineers and marketing are not especially good.

Turning market reports into requirements

Information collected by marketing is often not organized well enough to be useful to developers. Developers in turn have little respect for the faint voice of the customer that manages to come through. This is a pity as market requirements are necessary for products. Product managers can bridge this gap by transforming marketing knowledge into definite requirements.

4.3 User requirements in subsystem projects

This book focusses on user requirements. These are mostly but not always created outside subsystem projects and passed down to them. However, it does happen that subsystems find they need to do a little requirements engineering for themselves.

Subsystems inherit requirements, adding a few of their own

If your project is a subsystem – part of a larger system – don't expect to get many user requirements directly, although you may still have a few, such as on interfaces for testing or maintenance. If you have such an interface in your subsystem, you need to put together a miniature user requirements document, using the techniques described in this book. You will need to identify the users involved, discuss their needs, and perhaps see how they respond to a mock-up or prototype of the interface you propose to build.

However, the largest part of the task is to trace back to the requirements placed on your subsystem. These should ultimately trace back to the original user requirements. For example, if you are designing a database management module for a financial system, you must know the types and amount of information that need to be stored. If you are making the transmission for a car, you need to know how much power and consequently how much vehicle speed, vibration, and shock the subsystem has to handle. That figure is one of the end-to-end requirements that shape the whole design of the car.

The designers of subsystems need to understand the impact of what they are doing. Equally, if you are responsible for a system's specifications, you need to give each of your subsystem teams enough guidance on how their part fits into the bigger picture of what the users want.

5

Structuring the requirements

A medium-sized project typically needs hundreds of requirements. These can be fully understood only when they are organized logically. A good structure helps organize the requirements, making it easier to see what is necessary, where everything belongs, and how the different requirements fit together. It also makes the requirements easier to check for errors and omissions.

The best structure for user requirements follows the natural patterns of use, which is to say, the requirements should be written down in the order that their users would come to them in their work. Sometimes different orderings are possible, and sometimes there are alternatives and special cases. Each of these situations represents a scenario, which at its most basic is a sequence of goals for the users.

The requirements are therefore structured as a family of scenarios: each chapter, section, and subsection heading is the name of a goal or sub-goal. At the lowest level, each sub-subsection represents just one user task, and usually contains one functional requirement along with, typically, one or two constraints that apply to it.

5.1 You need structure as well as text

Everyday language is the only medium that users and developers share. However, text alone does not show how different user needs fit together. After all, you want to make a system, not a heap of unrelated functions. Therefore, you need to make a structure that will organize the requirements.

The structure must give readers a way into the text. A good structure shows the requirements at different levels of detail, and allows readers to focus on one section at a time. The users have to understand and feel that they own the user requirements, whoever wrote them. A combination of textual requirements and a scenario-like structure of section headings is effective because it is familiar, and it presents each requirement in exactly the place where the users would expect it. This arrangement can be supplemented by simple informal diagrams, as described in Chapter 3.

The aim is to show users just one simple structure, but to allow for any amount of detail. To do this, arrange what users need under chapter headings that represent the users' top-level goals. This list of goals is itself a scenario: if you step through them, you get an idea of what the whole problem is. Usually, the scenarios are simple sequences, one goal after another, but this is not the only possibility, as we will explain. The overall result is a hierarchy, but this is not necessarily reached by top-down analysis – users may instead volunteer whole scenarios, which you will have to fit together into a structure.

Users can then see the whole pattern before diving into the details. You probably need three levels of headings to organize the requirements: try not to use many more than that. Table 5.1 lists some common problems that affect requirement structure, and our suggested solutions.

TABLE 5.1 ■ Problems and solutions in structuring requirements

Problem	Solution
All readers need to understand the requirements	Write requirements in everyday language
Long lists of requirements are impossible to understand	Make a simple structure of chapters and sections to group the requirements
Requirements don't show what comes first	Organize the chapters and sections in time order so that they can be read as scenarios
Some requirements can be applied simultaneously, or in any order – a sequence is a needlessly tight ordering	Mark whether sections in the structure are sequences, parallels, or alternatives
The basic sequence of requirements doesn't show what to do if something goes wrong	Add a section for each exception, at the place where it could occur in the normal sequence
More than one sequence is possible in normal use	Describe all the sequences, mark them as alternatives
Some steps apply in several sequences	Describe them once, and reference them wherever needed
Some constraints apply to several requirements	If a constraint applies to a whole scenario, attach it to that section. If a constraint applies to separate sections, include cross-references
Users find it hard to get an overview of the whole document	1 All the above solutions 2 Add a simple informal diagram to support the text 3 Write an overview 4 Find out why they find it hard and restructure the document

5.2 Breaking down the problem into steps

Getting started with anything is proverbially harder than doing it. It is perfectly acceptable to make some mistakes when you first try to organize any set of requirements. As long as you know it is only a rough-cut of the final structure, you can ask users to help you improve it.

What is a goal?

A goal is a single desired result. There is a strong connection between goals and requirements: if you practice writing clear goals, you will have little difficulty expressing requirements. In your requirements documents, a single goal may be associated directly with one or several requirements (affordances) and constraints, whose purposes are to achieve the goal in the desired way.

Write down the goal

First, identify the goal for the whole problem. It helps to begin with the word "to," as this gets you thinking about a single action or mission. This is a natural way to phrase goals. For example, a goal for a cargo transportation enterprise might be *"to get the goods delivered."* A goal for an accounts office is *"to get payment for the company's products."*

People often leave out the word 'to' before their goals; it should be clear from the context whether a goal is intended. In the use case approach, the goal is the title of the use case, and it is not usual to prefix it with "to." This makes goals look like functions, which is natural – for example, getting the goods delivered is certainly a functional thing. The opposite would be to speak about an object like "goods delivery department." That is not a goal but an organizational structure or possibly a system. It would be wrong to talk about such objects in requirements before you know whether they will exist: you would be prejudging the system's design. So, keep your goals functional.

Write down the basic steps

Sometimes users will directly describe a scenario which you can treat as a sequence of steps to achieve a goal. Each step is in effect both a requirement (possibly at a high level) and a subgoal which you can use as a heading for a group of requirements. You may be able to prompt users simply by asking them to describe a real or imaginary scenario. Starting at the end – having reached the goal – and working backwards is sometimes the easiest approach. For example:

- to get payment into your company's account, you have to pay in the customers' checks;

- to get the checks, you have to send out invoices to the customers;

- to send the invoices, you obviously have to work out what they owe you;

- to work out …

It often helps to work backwards a step at a time in this way.

Some steps may involve the users in a large amount of work. Calculating the invoiced amount for an important customer may mean keeping a complete database covering orders, previous payments, discounts, state taxes, delivery charges, credit notes, and much more. You can repeat the process just explained, breaking down each step as if it was the goal.

Think about all the timescales involved

It may be necessary to consider different timescales to describe a problem properly. For an accounts department, the problem most likely divides naturally into separate orders placed by the customer. Or you could bill each customer monthly, in which case you'd collect up all the orders placed during the month, work out the monthly account details, and invoice the customer for that.

In the case of the sailboat example (Exercise 4: Extracting requirements from a memo), the likely timescale for a family sailing trip is a day. A scenario describing "a day in the life of" is often effective at eliciting requirements. More generally, a single use or mission, possibly longer than a day, may be a natural unit to consider.

A larger frame is the cradle-to-grave life cycle of the sailboat, from its manufacture, through distribution, sale, delivery, use and storage, repair, and finally disposal. Some requirements may apply only to one of these phases; for example, a constraint on the use of toxic materials may be of interest in the disposal phase.

Some services have to run continuously, such as a telephone network which is available to its subscribers 24 hours a day. However, you can still work with finite scenarios by thinking about transactions handled by the service from the user's point of view. The subscriber dials a number, is connected, has a conversation, and hangs up. Connection is plainly a set of transactions in its own right, but these are between switches and exchanges, with nowadays no human actors.

5.3 Organizing requirements into scenarios

We recommend that you organize the user requirements into operational scenarios. When you ask users what they do to reach a particular goal, they most often describe a simple sequence of activities. These represent the steps they would typically follow to achieve their goal. If the description is not clear to you, ask for an example, and the user will probably give you a more concrete scenario with names and places instead of generalizations.

Each step you identify can in its turn be taken as a more detailed goal, as already described, until you arrive at a structure with enough detail to put all the requirements in their natural places.

For a first-cut, assume that the steps form a single "normal business" sequence: a clear flow from first step to last. Users can think through the sequence as a scenario, and quickly detect gaps and errors. Later, you will add other sequences, such as exceptions. You may also identify alternative courses of action and sequences that users can carry out in parallel with each other. These will build more structure around the first-cut sequence. For example, you can expect emergency actions to branch off from the sequence of normal actions.

Goals, scenarios, requirements

We have already defined the terms **goal** – a single desired result – and **requirement** – a statement of need. These are closely related but not the same thing. A requirement can be constructed from a goal by adding at least two crucial pieces of information: who wants the result, and how important it is to them. In a requirements document, it seems natural to use the name of the goal as a section heading, and the requirement can then form the section text. In a requirements database or tool, the goal and requirement can form parts of the same information structure. Later, other pieces of information, attributes of the requirement, build it up further into a robust multi-purpose engineering component.

A **scenario** is something that can take many forms, from a storyboard presentation of a possible way of using a system to a concrete example of what users do in a certain situation. For our purpose here, we will define a scenario in a more abstract way as a sequence of steps taken by known types of user to achieve a goal. Each step in a scenario is a single activity taken to achieve a subgoal.

If you already have some scenarios which you have acted out with the users (Section 3.6), you can feed them directly into your structure. The kind of description from that activity – with preconditions, roles, and so on – is ideal for describing scenario steps.

To build the structure, start with the top-level goal – the end result that the user actually wants from using the system (Figure 5.1; the goal-word

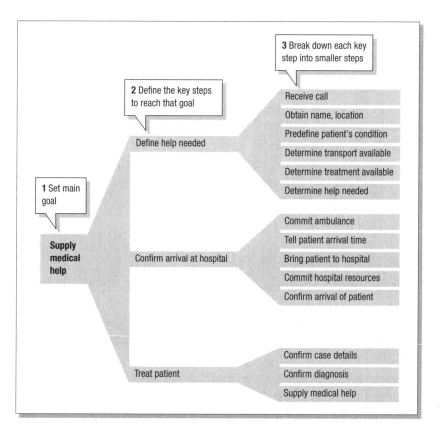

FIGURE 5.1 ■ Building the structure for user requirements

"to" has been omitted to keep the goals as short as possible). Then define the steps – subgoals – leading to that goal. Review the set of results that these high-level goals provide: are they what the users actually want?

Example: ambulance goals

In Figure 5.1, the results are that the patient's call is received, the aid needed by the patient is defined, the patient is taken to hospital, and the defined medical aid is supplied to the patient. Together, these results plainly do achieve the top-level goal, which is to help the patient to recover. How each of the results is to be achieved is not yet defined; but fortunately, even without that knowledge, users can agree with – or correct your understanding of – the goals.

The requirements, when you have written them (see Chapter 7), expand on the goals, stating precisely what the users want at each stage. For example, for the goal "commit ambulance," one of the requirements might be

"The ambulance controller shall be able to view the locations of available ambulances."

This helps the controller to commit the right transport, so the requirement can be seen to be in the right place. The requirement also helps to meet two constraints (see Section 6.2), namely to ensure that the patients are transported as quickly as possible, and to minimize the distance driven. Another requirement for the same goal might be

"The ambulance controller shall be able to commit an available ambulance to an incident."

Breaking down the goals

Once the high-level goals are agreed, decompose each of them into the sequence of smaller steps needed to reach the goal, and again check out your understanding with the users. Each step can then be treated as a subgoal and broken down in the same way, if necessary.

Sometimes several subgoals can be worked on simultaneously. For example, when a medical service has to respond to a major incident, three subgoals can be worked on in parallel, and none of them individually resembles the main goal:

Example: to prepare to treat patients in a major incident

To prepare to treat patients in a major incident (main goal):

- *summon backup medical staff to hospital (parallel step);*
- *prepare casualty department;* $\Big\}$ at once
- *summon backup ambulances to incident.*

Goals are not system objects

Note that describing a problem in terms of goals is not the same as assuming that the developers can solve the problem by treating each goal as a separate design object, and perhaps writing code for each one. Goals are held by users or other stakeholders. They do not necessarily relate directly to system functions or objects.

5.4 Examples of goal decomposition

Example: a customer billing system

To achieve the results the users want, ask the users to describe the steps leading up to their main goals. For example, in a customer billing system, the basic first-cut scenario could be like this:

To ensure the company's products or services are paid for (main goal):

- *Record the products or services supplied (sequential step).*
- *Calculate the cost.*
- *Prepare the bill for the customer.*
- *Send the bill.*
- *Receive payment (final step).*

Notice that the last step quite often, as here, shows that the main goal, the purpose of the system, has been reached. This is as it should be: getting that final result is what the system is all about. But it needn't be rigidly the same.

Thinking out the goals of a system is a powerful approach because it makes complicated problems seem simple. The users get to see a simple sequence of "results" which they can immediately understand, so they know what the system is all about from the start. Each result-along-the-way can in turn be taken as a goal. Working with the users, break down each goal into a sequence of smaller steps:

To calculate the cost (main goal):

- *[To] Find the unit cost of the individual products or services (step).*
- *[To] Find the net cost for the number of products supplied.*
- *[To] Find the gross cost including tax and delivery.*
- *[To] Find the billing amount including prepayment and interest.*

Notice how much easier it is to understand the problem when its steps are arranged in order. All of these steps probably need to be broken down in turn.

Example: repeated goals for an engine control system

Other kinds of problems lead to different lists of tasks. In an engine control system, the basic goal is:

To ensure power is available continuously (main goal):

- *[To] Monitor the engine with sensors (step).*
- *[To] Work out the desired engine state.*
- *[To] Compare the actual to the desired state.*
- *[To] Control the engine to the correct state.*

EXERCISE 5

A structure for user requirements

You are collecting the requirements for a utility company that serves many customers nationally. Customers call a head office on a toll-free number to place orders for service. The office dispatches mobile engineers from one customer to the next.

a Write down the purpose of the system as a goal. Keep this in mind as the result to be achieved by the end of the sequence you will be defining.

b Write down the basic steps, describing how the system operates, to form a scenario ending with the desired result from (a).

c Mark next to each step who does the work in that step. For example:

Receive service request from existing customer (actor: telephonist).

5.5 Handling exceptions

Exceptions to the "normal" events handled by a system that are missed in the requirements, and so not handled by the system, will probably cause system failures in operation. It is therefore vital to analyze the situations that users want to deal with before committing development resources to a project.

What is an exception?

An **exception event** is an unwanted event that takes a system out of its normal operating scenarios. It may be caused by something inside or outside the system.

An **exception scenario** defines the desired response to an exception event. It results in an end-state which is safe, and which is wherever possible back at some step in a normal scenario, so that users can continue with their work. In other words, the **goal** for an exception scenario is to handle the exception event safely. For example, if an order is received with no order number, it could simply be rejected; it would be better to handle the exception by trying to obtain a number, or perhaps by supplying a temporary one, to allow order processing to continue. The normal scenario – order is received, the number is entered into the database, the order goods are assembled... – is then resumed as if the exception had never occurred.

In other cases, you cannot resume completely normally until remedial action is taken. If there is a fire in an aircraft's engine, the immediate procedure is to cut off the fuel and extinguish the fire. With the engine safely stopped – one exception handled – the plane will continue to fly, but it is certainly going to land at the nearest suitable airfield instead of completing its flight as planned.

Analyzing exceptions

A baseline sequence of goals sets the scene for a project, defining the results users of a future system want it to achieve. For example, a billing system is there to bring in payments.

Example: getting a late payment

But what if a customer does not pay on time? The billing system successfully prepares and issues the right bill – and then nothing happens. The system will fail if it can't handle non-payment. Looked at as a user problem, non-payment is just another situation with a goal that has to be met. The goal is to handle the exception event: the payment didn't arrive. Just like a normal sequence goal, an exception-handling goal can be broken down into steps to form a scenario that sorts out the problem. For example:

To get a late payment (exception goal):

- *[To] Send a reminder bill (exception-handling step);*
- *[To] Receive payment;*
- *[To] Record when payment arrives;*
- *[To] Record payment received (final step of exception, back to normal).*

Notice that in this case the last step of the exception scenario shows that the exception has been handled successfully.

Analyze each exception goal you find in your system in the same way as you worked out the main goal: break it down into steps which lead to the result users want – the exception is handled safely. Each exception must link up with the main sequence as a branch from the place where the exception can occur. For instance, the need to collect a late payment can only be after the first bill has been sent out.

EXERCISE 6

Could anything go wrong here?

This exercise illustrates the need for requirements to handle exceptions. An example requirement suggests the operational context for each goal.

For each of the following goals (for different systems):

a Name an exception that could happen at that point.

b List the steps the users would have to take to handle the exception.

c Could more than one exception occur?

If so, name the additional exceptions.

d Can you think of ways to prevent any of the exceptions?

If so, write requirements or constraints for this purpose.

Notice that requirements and design are closely related here: try to avoid going into detail on the design.

1 Goal: To select a radio channel

Example requirement: The truck driver shall be able to select a radio channel by spoken command.

2 Goal: To prepare a sailboat for sailing

Example requirement: A crew of two persons aged at least seven shall be able to prepare the sailboat for sailing within ten minutes.

3 Goal: To drive on an icy surface

Example requirement: The driver shall be able to control the car on an icy surface at any speed up to 20 kilometers per hour.

4 Goal: To detect intrusion

Example requirement: The alarm shall sound within 30 seconds when an attempt is made to enter the protected house.

Finding out where exceptions can happen

Users may not immediately think of writing down what they want done when a problem arises. Ask them whether any exception can happen at each place in the requirement structure. Any place which can be affected by users or other systems is a likely candidate.

Some good questions to discover exceptions are:

"Can anything prevent you from reaching this goal?"

"Can anything go wrong here?"

"What else could happen when you are in this state?"

Example: goods not in stock

For example, an order-processing scenario may have a step "Fetch goods from warehouse," followed by packing and attaching the delivery note. If, despite a database check, one of the items is in fact unavailable – perhaps the warehouse stock item is damaged or wrongly labeled – then the order cannot be completed.

The exception can be handled by delaying the delivery and sending an urgent order to the item's manufacturer, or by printing a "part order" delivery note and arranging to send the missing item later. There may be many possible solutions once the need is identified.

Other exceptions may be possible for this step, and for the other steps in the scenario. For instance, the wrong delivery note might be attached to the packed goods.

Searching systematically for possible exceptions

It is a sad fact that few requirements documents show anything like a full evaluation of the exceptions that must be handled. In two areas – safety-critical systems, and user interface design – there is a tradition of good practice in identifying exceptions, under names such as hazard and fault tree analysis. Unfortunately, user error is not limited to filling in forms wrongly; mistakes can spread to affect all parts of a system, as can system failures.

The best hope is a systematic search for possible exceptions. For every step towards every goal, make sure that users have thought carefully about what could go wrong. Then they can consider whether their suggestions are important exceptions, and if so, how to mitigate them. Naturally, each new exception scenario they suggest creates more steps and more opportunities for exceptions, so the search takes time.

Exceptions

a Try to list all the exceptions that could arise when a plane lands. Consider the weather, the plane, the pilot, and the air traffic controller at least.

b Write user requirements to cover all your exceptions.

Alternatively, consider the exceptions that could arise at each step in one part of a project with which you are familiar. For example, what exceptions are possible in an e-commerce system where a customer is asked to complete and send in an electronic form including name, address, goods wanted, and payment details?

Exceptions drive the project cost

Make sure the user requirements cover all likely exceptions. Describing the ideal case when everything works is necessary, but not sufficient. Much of the cost of any complex system goes into making it dependable. Dependability is not solely an issue for safety-critical systems, where it is of course of the greatest importance. Any information system on which a business depends, such as a telephone utility company's call billing system, must itself be extremely reliable.

Creating a structure that caters for exceptions

After collecting user requirements from different sources, you need to sort them out so that they make sense and can be understood as a whole. The natural way to make the document do this is to attach the requirements to the goals in the basic scenario to deliver what users want, enhanced with extra scenarios — also broken into sequences of goals – to cope with exceptions. You'll know you have the structure right when users of any type instantly see how their goals and requirements fit into the whole thing.

By definition, an exception scenario is an alternative to a normal scenario, selected in response to an exception event. The main or "parent"

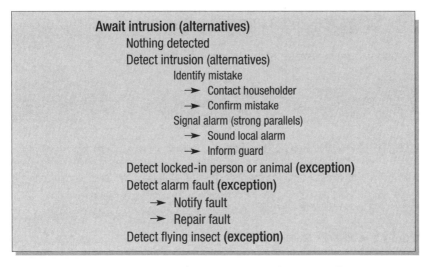

FIGURE 5.2 ■ Requirement subsections viewed as part of a scenario-like structure

goal where the exception can arise therefore always consists of a set of alternatives, at least one of which is a normal non-exception scenario; equally, there may be several exceptions, not only one. Identify where each required exception scenario fits into the structure and put it there (Figure 5.2). The illustrated structure also identifies a scenario that consists of a set of parallel subgoals, giving users and systems engineers a more precise description of the relationships between groups of requirements. For on-screen display, it is helpful to use colors as well as text labels to indicate goal type – for example, red for exceptions. In the use case approach, an exception can be treated either within a use case (as a local branch from the main scenario) or, if it is large enough, as a use case in its own right: it then has to be linked to the use case step(s) where it arose.

If there is still no appropriate section for a group of requirements, create one, and agree the change with the users. You should end up with at least one requirement for each goal.

5.6 Examples and exercises in requirement structure

Here are some examples for you to study and practice on.

Creating a heading structure

Work out a complete scenario-like heading structure to at least two levels, as illustrated in part in Table 5.2, for the user requirements document for a passenger aircraft.

TABLE 5.2 ■ Part of a scenario-like heading structure

1 Prepare aircraft for flight
1.1 Fueling
1.2 Cleaning
1.3 Loading baggage
1.4 Loading meals
2 Operate the flight
2.1 Taxiing to runway
2.2 Takeoff
2.3 Flight
2.4 Landing
2.5 Docking
3 Maintain aircraft
3.1 Daily servicing
3.2 Major servicing

EXERCISE 9

The right document for each subject

In the real world, requirements are sometimes confusingly organized. If you see a document like the one in Figure 5.3 you'll know you have some serious work to do.

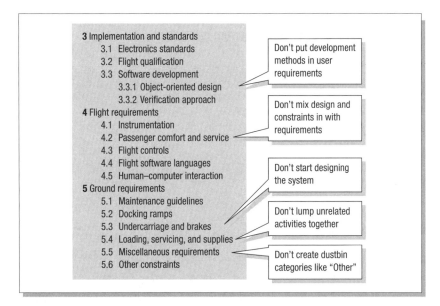

FIGURE 5.3 ■ How *not* to arrange your requirements

Work out which project document each of the headings in Figure 5.3 should be in.

Hint: likely candidates include the

- *user requirements;*

- *system specifications;*

- *system design;*

- *development plan; and*

- *maintenance plan.*

There may be others.

Wrongly placed requirements

Here are some requirements which do not belong together. You have been asked to organize them under the following section headings in the user requirements document. Identify the section where each requirement should actually go. Is there always a single right answer? Are the headings well chosen?

Sections in the proposed user requirements document

1   Preparation for flight.

2   Takeoff and landing.

3   Flight.

4   Maintenance.

5   Safety.

6   Performance.

7   Materials.

Flight requirements?

a   *All materials exposed externally shall be resistant to corrosion by salt-water spray. (Section   )*

b   *The aircraft shall be able to cruise at a steady airspeed of 800 kilometers per hour at 10,000 meters altitude. (Section   )*

c   *No failure in any one engine shall affect the operation of any other engine. (Section   )*

d   *Baggage handlers shall be able to push standard baggage carts directly into the cargo area. (Section   )*

e   *The pilot shall be able to dim the cabin lights for takeoff. (Section   )*

f   *The pilot shall be able to view the predicted time to landing. (Section   )*

g   *The pilot shall be warned if the undercarriage is not fully lowered during preparation for landing. (Section   )*

h   *Maintenance engineers shall be able to access all oil seals directly after removal of the engine covers. (Section   )*

i   *All materials used in the passenger compartment shall resist ignition under applied heat to FAA standard 123-45. (Section   )*

6

Requirements in context

A readable requirements document does not consist only of require-ments, no matter how clearly arranged. Technical documents should have a context; there are constraints on what can be done, and when; and there is an urgent need to keep track of requirement status, all the way through to completion.

In this chapter, we suggest some simple mechanisms for ensuring that your requirements work for you.

6.1 The user requirements document

Example structure

Table 6.1 shows a simple structure for a user requirements document, based on the European Space Agency's widely used Software Development Standards (Mazza, 1994).

TABLE 6.1 ■ A widely used structure for the user requirements document

1 **General description**	
1.1 Product perspective	
1.2 General capabilities	
1.3 General constraints	
1.4 User characteristics	
1.5 Operational environment	
1.6 Assumptions and dependencies	
2 **Specific requirements**	
2.1 Capabilities	– the scenarios
2.2 Constraints	– applying to the whole system

This structure allows you complete freedom to organize the requirements (affordances or capabilities) and constraints to explain the
problem as clearly as possible. Chapter 5 described a way of structuring the requirements; the question of the best way of organizing the
constraints is discussed below.

"Form follows function": make the document structure communi-cate effectively

Remember that the vital thing is to get the users' needs across to the
system designers. You can extend or modify a standard document as
long as you explain why you are doing so. If the standard you have to
use does not cover something you need, write a waiver and insert a
suitable document structure.

Requirements do not have to be arranged as traditional documents

Until requirements tools arrived, the only option available was for
requirements to be arranged in documents. As a result, most development standards assume that you will be controlling your requirements
purely with document structures. They therefore provide a hierarchy

of headings, with separate sections for items that are in fact closely related. For instance, the users may want a result within a certain time. Traditionally, this combination was expressed as a capability and a separate performance constraint. That arrangement made it hard to find or understand all the requirements related to the single desired result.

You are free to choose convenient information structures to suit the tools you have. An effective structure is a requirement object with a unique identifier, a text, an optional heading, and whatever attributes you need. In principle every capability (affordance) for the users comes with a desired performance, so a performance attribute may seem the logical choice. For instance, a bank may want to enable 1,000 customer transactions per second (tps). The performance, for example 1,000 tps, is an attribute of the capability, such as that each customer can query their own account.

6.2 Organizing the constraints

Many requirements are not capabilities but qualities of behavior that users want (user constraints), or that specialist engineers believe are necessary to enable systems to work satisfactorily (system constraints). These include safety, performance, reliability, testability, interoperability, and maintainability, among others. Systems engineers often call them simply the "-ilities".

Constraints can conveniently be kept with the capabilities that they apply to, or grouped by themselves if they apply to the whole system. Constraints occur in both user and system requirements, and most of this section applies to both kinds of requirement.

What is a constraint?

A **constraint** is a requirement that governs an aspect of a system other than what the system is to do. Informally, it narrows down the range of allowable solutions, constraining the system designers to work within a smaller solution space.

Local constraints govern single results; global constraints govern whole systems. For example, the performance constraint to answer incoming calls within five rings is local to one goal, namely to answer calls; but the constraint to deal with the problem raised by the customer in such a call within 48 hours is much wider, affecting many subgoals, and possibly global depending on the scope of the system.

Requirements that are not capabilities

Example: car transmission subsystem

Suppose you are working on a project to improve the transmission for a family car. The existing one works well enough, but to keep up with the market, the new version has to be quieter, more efficient, and therefore make the car more responsive, use less fuel, and be more comfortable and more reliable.

Constraints limit design options

There are probably few actual functions in your transmission subsystem: its purpose is to transmit power from the engine to the wheels. That's it, more or less. Think about what else the transmission has to do: for instance, power has to go to the wheels in the right ratio, however fast the car is going. But extras like this just limit the way you can design the transmission: the job has to be done in a certain way. The extra requirements are constraints. They are not less important than (sub)system functions, but they are different in nature. Constraints can be difficult to implement and to verify, as they often impinge on every part of a system.

Things that should not happen

There are other kinds of constraints. For example, the transmission must not create a fire hazard; if there isn't enough oil pressure, the driver should know quickly. These requirements do not affect the basic purpose of the subsystem, but they greatly affect how it can be designed and made. Constraints make up most of the requirements for some systems. As they often need to be worked on by different people, find a way of organizing them which is helpful to your project.

Existing interface and environmental constraints

Any real system works within an operational environment. If we build a payroll system, it works with the existing financial control system. If we build a plane, it has to interact with existing radar systems and airports. The operational environment puts many constraints on the new system.

Safety constraints

Safety requirements are important constraints. The safety team has to work out all the hazards and faults which could threaten safety. They do this by analyzing the functions, and later the design, of a system. They consider how likely each hazard is, what can be done to reduce the risk that it will happen to an acceptable level, and what to do if it happens. They also combine all the hazards to estimate how safe the whole system is. Now this is a specialized task. Obviously, it is a good idea to keep safety requirements in a separate chapter or document, so the safety engineers can work on them while the system designers work on the system itself.

Performance constraints

Quantifying the capabilities for a user transaction

Performance requirements powerfully constrain system design. They typically quantify the value of capabilities (affordances). For example, we may want a certain power level (in telecommunications), or to be able to perform so many user transactions per second (in banking, for instance). The performance constraint is often a numeric attribute of a capability, or (perhaps more typically) of a complete transaction or operational scenario. For example, if you have a transmitter and a receiver, the key performance constraint is likely to be the bandwidth between the two functions:

The channel shall be able to handle 100 kilobits per second.

This is common to the transmitting and receiving steps which are part of the same scenario. If you duplicate the constraint, there is a danger that one of the copies may be changed, creating an inconsistency. It would be better to link the constraint to both steps, but this still does not allow for the possibility that other behaviors may be added, for example, error correction or encryption on the channel. The constraint should therefore be applied to the whole scenario: all steps in that scenario have, together, to comply.

Budgeting to meet end-to-end system constraints

In the corresponding system specification, the constraint will be translated into a single performance budget, shared out among the system functions. The need to budget logically traces back to a single constraint on the channel's performance. The way the budget is shared depends on the system engineer's understanding of the system design: specification and design influence each other. Trade-offs usually have to be made between them and also with the user requirements, as the development team works out what can be done realistically within the schedule and cost constraints on the project. The users may be asked to decide whether to accept a system that delivers slightly less performance than anticipated but which can be delivered on time and to cost.

Performance constraints often apply across whole systems

If the transmission has to be 15% more efficient, i.e. to deliver 15% more of the input power to the wheels than the old model, which component has to be improved? Very probably all of them, so the constraint is system-wide.

You need to make sure your readers see at once that the end-to-end performance constraints apply to the whole system. Other kinds of constraint which are often like this include cost, reliability, maintainability, and environmental, as well as physical, considerations such as size, weight, and non-toxicity.

Not reliability but dependability

Requirements of any of these kinds usually make sense only for a system as a whole. The driver of a car is not necessarily interested in the reliability of individual engine components; the key requirement is the ability of the car to make the next journey successfully. This user-level constraint is sometimes known as 'dependability' to distinguish it from component qualities such as reliability or availability. Users want results, not components or even systems.

Where to put constraints

Separate or merge

There are two opposite approaches to placing constraints: either in a separate group from other requirements, or merged with the capabilities to which they apply. Safety constraints, for example, are often organized in a separate section, typically the responsibility of a safety team. The opposite approach would attach a safety constraint and a safety classification to each capability or group of capabilities.

The separate approach has the merit of making it easy to find and compare all the constraints. The merged approach has the merit of making it easy to see the relationship of each capability to each constraint.

The polarization between the two approaches is no longer as sharp as it was. This is firstly because requirements tools enable requirements to be selected on any desired set of criteria. For example, a safety officer could see the safety-critical requirements by filtering with the criterion *Safety Class = "Critical."* Secondly, requirements tools allow a constraint to be linked to other requirements and then viewed with them. Different "virtual" documents can be presented to different people, and printed out as actual documents when necessary.

Global and local constraints

As for positioning constraints within a user requirements document, there are three basic possibilities which are worth spelling out.

1   Constraint is local to one lowest-level goal. It can be written as:

- a separate requirement after the capability (or affordance) for that goal. This creates a text which can easily become repetitive, because of the need for each requirement to stand alone. For example:

  The controller shall be able to cancel an order.

  The controller shall be able to cancel an order up to 30 minutes after it has been issued;

- an attribute of the capability requirement. This creates a compact table or object structure in place of a traditional text. A variant of this is to use a single object for the lowest-level goal, its capability, and constraints on it. Performance constraints are well handled in this way; for example, the constraining phrase *"within five seconds"* can be placed beside the requirement to which it applies, avoiding repetition;

- a separate requirement, placed anywhere in the document, linked to the capability. This creates a group of capabilities and a cross-reference table. The structure is difficult to read unless a requirements tool is used to create views presenting the constraints together with linked requirements.

2 **Constraint is local to a high-level goal**, covering a group of related capabilities (or affordances). It can be written as:

- a separate requirement in the section representing the goal. For example, if a customer's bill is to be prepared every month, that constraint can be placed directly in the section headed by the goal "[To] Prepare Bill." It then applies implicitly to all the capabilities in that section, including calculating the cost of the services provided;

- an attribute of the goal which heads the section. This is consistent with the merged approach for constraints applying to individual capabilities;

- a separate requirement, placed anywhere in the document, linked to the goal or to each of the capability requirements grouped under the goal. There seem to be few advantages to this option.

3 **Constraint is global**, applying to the whole system. It can be written as:

- a separate requirement in a global constraints chapter. This creates a traditional text structure as in Table 6.1;

- an attribute of the top-level goal for the whole system. This is consistent with the merged approach for local constraints.

These three kinds of constraint are illustrated in Figure 6.1.

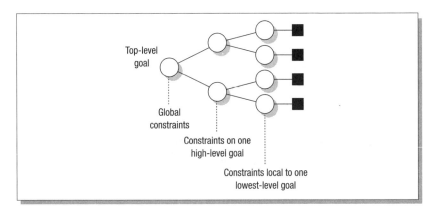

FIGURE 6.1 Types of constraint

We suggest you use either an attribute approach throughout, at least for specific types of constraint such as performance, or a separate constraint requirement approach throughout. Global constraints present the least difficulty, whether they have a separate section or are placed under the top-level goal. Constraints local to one lowest-level goal are probably best placed close to that goal. The positioning of constraints local to a high-level goal that represents a group of capabilities is more controversial, but it seems sensible to make your approach consistent. Above all, choose an approach that the stakeholders find readable.

EXERCISE 11

Writing constraints

- Define the levels of dependability users require of a system you are familiar with, or of a truckers' mobile communications system.

- Write the safety constraints for the people who clean the windows of a 100-story building.

- Write the performance constraints for the people who clean the windows of a 100-story building. (*Hint: how long should it take them to reach a window on the 50th floor?*)

6.3 Defining the scope

Projects succeed only when they know what they have to accomplish. It is vital to define from the start exactly what your system does and does not have to cover. This is known as the system's scope.

Agree on exactly what to include

Scope is critical

A clear view about what to include is critical. All too often there is confusion about whether something is in or out of a system. For example, users may have legitimate requirements that are impossible to meet in the time available, or which are seen as too expensive by the customer. As a result, the system's scope has to be cut down to ensure success.

Scope is defined by negotiation

The scope of any system is defined by negotiation between the customer, who states what is needed from a business perspective, and the developer, who says what is practical. Users, who may have a technical or practical perspective, predictably want more than the customer is willing to pay for. Make sure you know who has the final say on system scope.

Identify priorities

The best approach to scoping is for the customer to state upfront what is needed, even before the requirements are collected. Of course, the customer must never stop users asking for what they want, even if some items are slightly out of scope. That does not mean that those requirements will never be implemented. Keep them, but mark them as "to be implemented later" – in other words, give them a priority. (See Section 6.4 for how to manage status information with requirement attributes.) This is far better than deleting requirements, only to have them re-introduced and re-argued at the next review meeting.

Work out what can be afforded

It is a rare project that experiences no tension between what the users would like and what the customer is willing to pay for. The key to success is to make realistic estimates of cost, to prioritize the requirements, and then to make sensible trade-offs.

Meeting budget constraints

When a system has to be limited in scope because a requirement cannot be met with the available budget, the first rule is not to despair: developers can often suggest simpler alternatives which will do 80% of what the users wanted.

Once the customer has made clear how much they can afford, developers and users can sit down with the requirements and work out how to get as much as possible done within the budget. They may well be able to implement several of the "to be implemented later" requirements in a modified form. Equally, some of the planned items may be found to be too costly and have to be deferred.

Getting 80% of what you want

For example, a requirement to provide voice-command radio cut-off for the truck driver may be troublesome for the developers, as it demands sophisticated signal processing to handle the many possible nuances of speech. But the developers may be able to arrange a simple and cheap cut-off when the speech signal comes to an end. This probably meets most of the intention of the requirement at a fraction of the price – and it can be done at once. Obviously it is vital to agree any such compromises in advance.

Make a definite decision

When there are competing pressures on time, money, staff, and other resources – and there always seem to be – you have to reach a clear decision on how to proceed. Decision support is outside the scope of this book, but there are well-documented techniques and tools that make the job of making decisions a little easier.

EXERCISE 12

Restricting the scope

For your own system, define two requirements which the user would like, but which the customer and the developer have restricted.

	Original requirement	Restricted requirement	Why was it restricted?
Example	The CEO's car shall be 100% available, seven days a week	A suitable car shall be available to the CEO, seven days a week	Need for maintenance means one specific car cannot meet this requirement
1			
2			

6.4 Requirement attributes

Requirements are engineering objects and must be organized and tracked as such. Status and related information is best held in the form of requirements database attributes.

Status information is essential

Up to now, this book has described requirements as if they were just pieces of text, probably single sentences containing the word "shall" and as few other words as possible. This is fine as far as it goes, but it is not the whole story. Each requirement needs to contain status values as well as text. Requirements are engineering objects in their own right – powerful ones, because they influence everything in the project.

Requirements are more than pieces of text

A warehouse containing engineering parts, such as components of a jet engine, does not consist of a heap of turbine blades sitting on shelves. Each part is carefully cataloged. The staff can check exactly when each one was manufactured, by which organization, in which batch, and what its part number and unique serial number are. The parts are permanently marked so that they can be identified and traced.

In the same way, a set of requirements must not be just a pile of requirement texts. Each requirement is unique, was written by someone at a particular time, may have been modified similarly, may have been reviewed, and should have a priority.

A complete requirement consists of a text and all of this status information. The need to track the status of requirements is an argument for tool support (Figure 6.2), as is the need to trace requirements to implementation and tests.

A document outliner can handle a hierarchy of requirements. An ordinary relational database can handle a table of information, such as the status of a set of requirements. A well-designed requirements tool must do both of these and more.

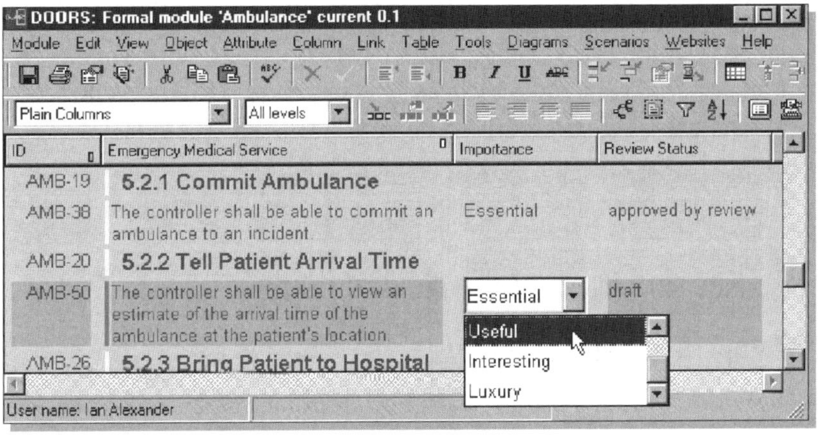

FIGURE 6.2 ■ Requirements status recorded in attributes

Checklist: recording source, status, and associated constraints

Here is a checklist of actions to enable people on your project to track the source and status of your requirements. The values attached to each requirement are most easily handled with a requirements tool which provides full industrial-strength handling of attributes.

- Record who suggested the requirement, when, and where. For example, insert a reference to the original text or tape.

- Record how far the requirement is towards being accepted, choosing from an enumeration such as {proposed, reviewed, accepted, rejected, to be modified}.

- Record how urgently the requirement is wanted, from an enumeration such as {essential, useful, interesting, luxury}.

- Record the requirement's priority in the development of any future system, by specifying the required date or release number.

- Identify how the requirement will be verified, choosing from an enumeration such as {test, demonstration, simulation, inspection, analysis}.

- Record any constraints that apply specifically to this particular requirement, such as safety, performance, or reliability. (Constraints that apply to several requirements or to whole scenarios are better represented by separate items, linked as necessary.)

- Record any numeric values that must be budgeted for, such as mass/weight, power consumption, network bandwidth, transaction time. (You may need to use pairs of attributes: one for the target value, one for the achieved value.)

- Record any questions against the requirement.

6.5 Keeping track of the requirements

The importance of traceability

Stakeholders say what they want in requirements. They can only be sure they get it by verifying that each requirement has been met. To do this, the acceptance tests must trace back to the requirements, covering all of them appropriately. Incidentally, scenarios of interest to users are good candidates for acceptance test scripts.

Similarly, the developers can only be sure they are implementing all the requirements if they can ultimately – though not necessarily directly – trace each design element back to the requirements concerned, and check that each requirement is fully covered. They can also use traces in the other direction to show that each design element is actually called for in the requirements. The management of traces between engineering objects such as requirements, tests, and design elements is called traceability (Figure 6.3). It is a vital tool in managing system development through requirements.

Forces of change

Getting an agreed and signed-off requirements document is an important milestone in every project. But it does not mark the end of the need for you and the users to keep an eye on the requirements.

New requirements and design possibilities emerge. A new technology may make some requirements easier to implement. A competitor may add a critical feature that demands a quick response. Customers' expectations of systems and user interfaces rise. Other apparent changes may in fact not be new but were missed during requirements capture.

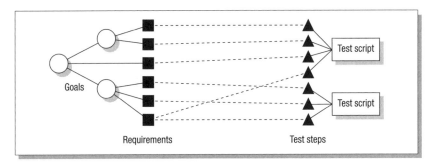

FIGURE 6.3 ■ Traceability demonstrates coverage of requirements by objects that trace to them, such as test steps or design elements

Risks to projects

There are many other forces trying to blow your project off course. Schedules change; staff join and need to be trained, or leave, taking all their knowledge and experience of the project with them, or fall ill, or take holidays. Organizations such as suppliers reorganize, merge, are taken over, and go bankrupt, usually just when you most need them. Offices are relocated, disrupting your infrastructure and carefully optimized network architecture. Back at home, people make mistakes, or forget requirements, or misinterpret the carefully worded text. Systems engineers are, after all, only human. Any of these risks could force you to compromise on the requirements and implementation.

Tracking change

As a result of these risks, you constantly need to check for changes in the design and requirements, just to keep up. To do this, you have to trace from each requirement to the design component that satisfies it. You have to check that the design is in fact sufficient to meet the requirement.

Example: trucker communications

For example, to satisfy the requirement that truckers can safely contact customers while on the move, the design could call for a headset with microphone. This certainly allows truckers to listen and talk while driving, but it does not offer a solution to the need to make contact.

That could be done with a hands-free dialing system, which might be voice-operated. If voice technology improves enough to make that option cost-effective, the truckers might demand the previously impossible – fully hands-free operation.

This example also illustrates an important point: a requirement may need several design solutions. A single design element can sometimes satisfy several requirements, so the traceability relationships between requirements, design elements, and test steps can quickly get complicated.

Advantages of using a requirements tool

A requirements tool such as the one shown in Figure 6.4 can help you check that there is at least one trace from each requirement to the design: if there are any untraced requirements, there is work to be done. But it can't check that the traced parts of the design are sufficient or correct – that's your job. The illustration shows a traceability column set up on the right of the requirement text. There may be any number of links between requirements and system or test specifications: each linked item is in this case shown as an identifier and a text. The requirement's own identifier is shown on the left; this could if desired be displayed in the system specifications in a column labeled something like "Original user requirement." All the column layouts can be customized to suit the needs of individual projects.

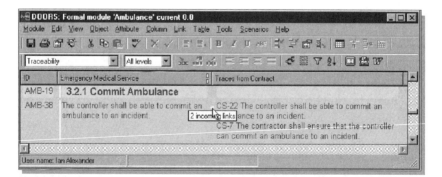

FIGURE 6.4 ■ Traces displayed in a dynamically updated column beside the requirements in a commercial requirements tool

Handling traceability and change without a requirements tool is tedious, and it is easy to make mistakes. The design changes quite often and requirements need to be updated as well. On any but the smallest project, tracing requires reliable, industrial-strength tool support. To keep track of changes by hand means recording in a table each change to each requirement, each design element, and each test, and checking each time via a traceability matrix for any possible impact on other items. If you need to trace directly to design, a requirements tool that can interface directly with your design tool is virtually essential.

7

Requirements writing

Well-written requirements prevent common but serious problems. The basic goal is clarity; if there is one thing that makes for good requirements, it consists of not attempting to do too much. If you have created and agreed a good structure then the individual requirements should fall into place without difficulty. When a particular requirement proves to be awkward to write, it is likely that the structure needs to be developed a stage further to break down the requirements into simple statements of need. This chapter offers some practical guidelines and examples.

7.1 Quality, not perfection

Requirements are often stated badly initially and you have to work on them to find out what is really wanted, and to rewrite them so that they are clear and precise. We certainly don't believe you can write "the perfect requirement" – there is no such thing.

7.2 Sketch, then improve

Expect requirements to improve as you and the users think about what is wanted, and you reflect on how to express the need as clearly as possible. There is no need to try to get the wording perfect the first time.

Some requirements engineers follow a deliberate strategy of writing down sketches of their newly captured requirements. If you label such drafts as "Rough Sketch," there is no danger of confusion. Then you can freely jot down what you feel to be the users' intentions, leaving until later a full analysis of the implied requirements. You then need to discuss the requirements with their owners, before formal review.

7.3 Anatomy of a good requirement

To some extent, user requirements can be analyzed to check whether their structure is acceptable. Each user requirement should have a

- user type who benefits from the requirement;
- defined desirable state for the user to reach, often an Object with a Qualifier;
- mechanism to allow a test to be written against the requirement.

Components of an imaginary requirement in traditional style

User type:	The call center operator ...
Result type (verb):	... shall be able to view ...
Object:	... details of a protected household ...
Qualifier (adverbial phrase):	... within two seconds of issuing a query.

The box above shows an imaginary requirement dissected into component parts. The call center operator is the user type. The "state" that the operator reaches is to have viewed the details of the household protected by one of the company's alarms. The requirement is clearly measurable.

The box overleaf shows another example, from quite a different domain. Whatever you require, the structure of individual written requirements is much the same. Notice that the sentence structure is

Components of a pilot's requirement in present-tense style

User type:	The pilot ...
Result type (verb):	... controls ...
Object:	... the aircraft's angle of climb ...
Qualifier (adverbial phrase):	... with one hand.

shorter and simpler with a present-tense verb ("...controls...") in place of the traditional "shall." The "shall" can readily be replaced by a value such as "Essential" in an Importance attribute of the requirement.

7.4 Guidelines for good requirements

Here are some simple guidelines with examples which we hope are reasonably clear. We do not believe that there can be a perfect set of universally applicable guidelines, any more than perfect requirements, but if you are getting started in the field you may find them useful.

Use simple direct sentences

Every requirement should be a single active sentence, as short as possible – but no shorter.

Example: *The pilot shall be able to view the airspeed.*

Use a limited vocabulary

Write in a simple subset of English, avoiding terms that may confuse non-technical or foreign readers.

Example: *The airline shall be able to change the aircraft's seating from business to holiday charter use in less than 12 hours.*

There is no need to use big words such as "reconfigure;" no need to use acronyms like FAA, abbreviations like "pax," or industry jargon such as "Conventional GlobalBusiness/GlobalTraveller seating configuration." On the other hand, when there is a technical term that concisely expresses your intended meaning, use it.

Identify the type of user who wants each requirement

Every requirement should start by naming a class of user.

Example: *"The navigator shall be able to ..."*

Focus on stating results

Every requirement should name a single desired result. In a capability or affordance, this is something to be provided to the named class of user.

Example: *"...view storm clouds by radar ..."*

Define verifiable criteria

Every requirement must be verifiable. Often you can indicate a possible test by adding a simple phrase to qualify a basic need. Later you will connect a specific acceptance criterion with the requirement text.

Example: *"... at least 100 kilometers ahead"*

Acceptance criterion: *Aircraft flying at 800 km/hour at 10,000 meters towards a known storm cloud indicated by meteorology satellite report; storm cloud is detected at a range of at least 100 km.*

You do not necessarily have to write acceptance test criteria while you are preparing user requirements, but you should be sure that practical tests, or other ways of verifying your requirements, can be devised readily. If it isn't verifiable, it isn't a requirement.

Suzanne Robertson talks, in slightly different language, about "fit criteria" – how well a solution fits the requirement: system designers can use the criteria to satisfy themselves that they have found a solution acceptable to users (Robertson, 1999). In Robertson's method, every requirement contains not only a textual description of the user's intention but also a fit criterion. This strict approach means more effort while writing, but promises fewer problems later in the project.

User requirements may be clear but hard to verify. For example,

"The crew find the sailboat fun to sail"

could in principle be tested in a series of trials using representative volunteers of different ages and levels of experience. The acceptance criterion might be that the average enjoyment score is over 50%. This is a feasible approach, and though it might be costly in practice, testing is usually cheaper than making a product that does not attract users.

7.5 Don't write like this

There are many ways of losing control of a project through bad requirements. Here are some things to avoid. None of the rules are absolute – you can probably make up examples where each of the danger signs is reasonable in a requirement – but the rules may be helpful when you are getting started.

Avoid ambiguity

Avoiding ambiguity is one of the most subtle and difficult issues in writing requirements. Try to write clearly and explicitly, but don't take this too far or your text will become unreadably boring and other people will fail to improve it. Although this book emphasizes structure and written expression of requirements, informal text, scribbled diagrams, conversations, and phone calls are excellent ways of removing ambiguity.

Dangerous ambiguities can be caused by the word "**or**," but also by many more subtle errors.

Example: *"The same subsystem shall also be able to generate a visible or audible caution/warning signal for the attention of the co-pilot or navigator."*

Which subsystem? Is the signal to be visible, audible, or both? Is it both caution and warning, just caution, or just warning? Is it for both the co-pilot and the navigator, or just one of them? If just one of them, which one and under what conditions?

Don't make multiple requirements

Requirements which contain conjunctions – words that join sentences together – are dangerous. Problems arise when readers try to puzzle out which part applies, especially if the different clauses seem to conflict, or if the individual parts apply separately.

Dangerous conjunctions include: **and, or, with, also**.

Example: *"The battery low warning lamp shall light up when the voltage drops below 3.6 volts, and the current workspace or input data shall be saved."*

How many requirements is that? What should be saved, and when?

Don't build in let-out clauses

Requirements which contain let-outs are dangerous. They look as though they are asking for something definite, but at the last moment they back down and allow for other options. Problems arise when the requirements are to be tested and someone has to decide what, if anything, could prove the requirement was not met.

Dangerous let-outs include: **if, when, but, except, unless, although**. The word **always** often introduces a let-out.

Examples: *"The forward passenger doors shall open automatically when the aircraft has halted, except when the rear ramp is deployed."*

"The fire alarm shall always be sounded when smoke is detected, unless the alarm is being tested or the engineer has suppressed the alarm."

There are two or more scenarios in both these examples. The let-outs are trying to cover alternative cases. These would be better handled as separate requirements under separate headings.

Don't ramble

Long rambling sentences quickly lead to confusion and error.

Example: *"Provided that the designated input signals from the specified devices are received in the correct order where the system is able to differentiate the designators, the output signal shall comply with the required framework of section 3.1.5 to indicate the desired input state."*

Don't design the system

Requirements specify the design envelope, and if we supply too much detail we start to design the system prematurely, especially when they come to our favorite areas. Danger signs include: **names of components, materials, software objects/procedures, database fields**.

Example: *"The antenna shall be capable of receiving FM signals, using a copper core with nylon armoring and a waterproof hardened rubber shield."*

Specifying design rather than actual need often increases the cost of systems by placing needless constraints on development and manufacture. Design constraints are sometimes necessary, but not as often as some requirements writers seem to think. For example, an aircraft component manufacturer had long had great difficulty and expense making a specific part, which was basically a cylinder with some machined grooves. A hole had to be drilled near one end, precisely 90° from a groove at the other end. One day the firm's production director was touring the engine maker's factory. He saw for the first time how the component was being used: the hole was just for a fixing pin. The alignment didn't matter much. Production costs tumbled.

Knowing why is much better than *knowing what.*

Don't mix requirements and design

The user requirements form a complete model of what users want. They need to be organized coherently to see gaps and overlaps. The same applies to system specifications – they form a complete model of the proposed system. A quick road to confusion is to mix up user requirements, system specifications, design elements, test cases, development guidelines, and installation instructions. Danger signs are references to **system, design, testing,** or **installation**.

Example: *"The user shall be able to view the currently selected channel number which shall be displayed in 14pt Swiss type on an LCD panel tested to Federal Regulation Standard 567-89 and mounted with shockproof rubber washers."*

At the least, this mixes a capability or affordance with a display constraint. The choice of an LCD panel can probably be left until system design. The mounting suggests that the LCD panel might have been chosen for ruggedness, in which case that should be a constraint. The panel is probably to be used to display more than just the channel number, so the display requirements should be in a separate section.

Don't mix requirements and plans

Another easy route into trouble with requirements is to mix up requirements and plans or schedules. Plans are essential, but they do not belong in the requirements. Usually they are updated throughout the project, whereas the requirements should stabilize. Mixing requirements with plans tends to increase the requirements workload through extra revisions and review meetings. Danger signs are references to **dates**, **project phases**, and **development activities**.

Example: *"The channel display type – LCD, LED, or TFT – shall be selected by 15 March and the first prototype panel shall be available for testing by the start of phase 3."*

Don't speculate

Requirements are part of a contract between customer and developer, with users as interested third parties. There is no room for "wish lists" – general terms about things that somebody probably wants. Danger signs include vagueness about *which* type of user is speaking, and generalization words: **usually**, **generally**, **often**, **normally**, **typically**.

Example: *"Users normally require early indication of intrusion into the system."*

Don't play on ambiguous requirements

Some constructions, such as the use of "or" and "unless" in requirements, allow different groups of readers to understand different things from the same wording. It is possible to use this technique deliberately: a development manager could attempt to postpone, until too late, any possibility of the customer's asking for what was wanted, while a customer could hope to mislead the supplier into offering to complete a job at a lower price, thinking that the requirement was less demanding than it really was. This practice is dangerous whoever attempts it, and can easily backfire.

Example: *"Operators shall be able to back up any disk on to a high-speed removable disk drive or tape cartridge."*

This could be interpreted to mean "a high-speed drive, or a high-speed tape cartridge," which is presumably what the users want; it could also mean "a high-speed drive, or any sort of tape cartridge," which might be cheaper for the developer to supply if the users' wishes can be ignored.

The only approach which works is for everyone to make requirements as clear as possible, and for all stakeholders to co-operate. In the long run, project success is in everybody's interest.

Don't use vague, undefinable terms

Many words used informally to indicate desired qualities are too vague for use in requirements.

Vague terms include: **user-friendly, versatile, flexible, approximately, as possible, efficient, improved, high performance, modern**.

Requirements using these terms are unverifiable because there is no definite test to show whether the system has the indicated property.

Examples: *"The print dialog shall be versatile and user-friendly."*

"The OK status indicator lamp shall be illuminated as soon as possible after the system self-check is completed."

Don't express possibilities

Possibilities are indicated with terms such as: **may, might, should, ought, could, perhaps, probably**. If developers do only what they have to, they will always ignore things that users might possibly require.

Example: *"The reception subsystem probably ought to be sensitive enough to receive a signal inside a steel-framed building."*

Avoid wishful thinking

Engineering is a real-world activity. No system or component is perfect. Wishful thinking means asking for the impossible. Developers will rightly query or reject wishful requirements. Wishful terms include: **100% reliable. Safe. Handle all unexpected failures. Please all users. Run on all platforms. Never fail. Upgradable to all future situations**.

Examples: *"The gearbox shall be 100% safe in normal operation."*

"The network shall handle all unexpected errors without crashing."

Good requirements

Analyze the following list of "user" requirements. Are they clear and verifiable? If not, reformulate them into proper user requirements, or say what kind of requirements they are.

"The communication system shall break down no more than twice per year."

"The system shall be easy to use by personnel with minimal training."

"The average delay to the user caused by the motorway toll system shall be less than 15 seconds."

"All users shall use the same commercial software for project management."

"The maximum delay between transmission and reception of an invoice shall be two hours."

"The database shall store ten years of records."

"The call dispatcher shall be able to communicate by radio to the ambulance driver."

Writing requirements for familiar domestic systems

Consider the following domestic design problems. Then think about what the designers were trying to do, and write what you consider to be the correct user requirements for a refrigerator, toaster, and burglar alarm.

We have suggested some solutions to the first one: can you improve on these?

Example 1: The refrigerator

Domestic refrigerators typically have a control, inside the food compartment, labeled 1-2-3-4-5. "5" instructs the refrigerator to apply maximum effort to cool the food.

Problems with this design:

■ In summer, a setting of "5" causes the food to stay fresh; in winter the food often freezes at this setting.

- In winter, a setting of "1" causes the food to stay fresh; in summer, the food is likely to spoil rapidly at this setting.

What is the real user requirement for a refrigerator?

"The user specifies the temperature at which the food is to be maintained"

seems to be the gist, but what about

"The food compartment is maintained at a temperature low enough for safe food storage"?

And possibly also:

"The user specifies the temperature without opening the food compartment"

while the following may be a requirement as well:

"The user observes the actual temperature of the food compartment."

Complete the list with what you consider to be the real user requirement for a refrigerator.

Example 2: The toaster

Domestic toasters typically have a steel casing, surrounding the heating elements, and a spring-loaded bread slice holder. The holder operates a switch that disconnects the power when it springs up; the spring is released by a timer; the timer is set by the user.

Problems with this design:

- The casing can become dangerously hot.
- The degree of cooking and burning of the toast depends on
  - how much water it contained at the start;
  - how hot the toaster was at the start, and
  - how thick the slice of bread was.
- The power is not disconnected if the toast warps and jams the spring-loaded holder, so the toast can catch fire.

What is the real user requirement for a toaster?

Example 3: The burglar alarm

Domestic burglar alarms typically consist of several sensors, such as movement detectors, door position detectors, and pressure switches, connected to a control box that sets off the alarm when any sensor reports intrusion.

Problems with this design:

■ Single sensors have quite a high false-positive failure rate, as when an insect flies near a movement detector. The police observe that 99% of alarm calls are false, and therefore often ignore them.

■ Simple alarms continue ringing until stopped manually. The police now prosecute householders who allow alarms to ring for more than 20 minutes.

What is the real user requirement for a burglar alarm?

EXERCISE 15

Ambiguous requirements

Busy people can easily find themselves writing contorted and ambiguous requirements. Here are two examples.

1 The system shall perform at the maximum rating at all times except that in emergency it shall be capable of providing up to 125% rating unless the emergency continues for more than 15 minutes, in which case the rating shall be reduced to 105%, but in the event that only 95% can be achieved then the system shall activate a reduced-rating exception and shall maintain the rating within 10% of the stated value for a minimum of 30 minutes.

2 The system shall provide general word-processing facilities which shall be easy to use by untrained staff and shall run on a thin Ethernet Local Area Network wired in the overhead ducting with integral interface cards housed in each system together with additional memory if that should prove necessary.

■ Try to work out what the authors of these two requirements must have intended, and redraft these intentions as better user requirements.

Hint: look for conjunctions, let-out clauses, untestable demands, physical layout, and design details.

■ What additional information would you need to make good requirements in these cases? Who would you need to consult?

8

Checking and reviewing

N o-one ever managed to write a brilliant user requirements document in one session. The requirements process is not complete until the users have thoroughly checked all aspects of their requirements. Once that has been done, and their comments have been incorporated in an agreed way, the requirements are ready for formal review. This is not simply a way of checking the document again, it is a crucial step in obtaining agreement on what is to be developed and what is not. Review always involves the customer who will pay for the development, as well as the other stakeholders who may be more closely concerned with day-to-day use.

This chapter looks at how to check the document structure and the requirements, and then at the process of formal review.

8.1 Checking the document structure with users

Once you have established a basic structure, take it back to the users and check it out. The purpose of the structure is to help organize the requirements. The reason for taking the trouble to organize them is to make it easier to see what is necessary, where everything belongs, and how the different requirements fit together. The users in particular are the people who must decide whether the structure represents the correct framework for their requirements. All the stakeholders should be invited to participate in the review process, even if they are not users themselves.

Let users check the document structure

Allow users time to check out the requirements structure so that it makes sense to them. You can't just leave a document with users and hope they will find all the mistakes. Checking is an active task which requires users to understand the proposed structure, and to think through each sequence of activities. You can encourage and assist them with these tasks, either in workshops or in individual review sessions. Don't take their comments as criticism: what they say now is improving the system.

Getting the most out of walkthroughs and inspections

Your goal is to iron out all the wrinkles in the proposed structure so that it fits the users' problem exactly. To do this, bring the structure to life for users with walkthroughs or inspections. They will give you feedback as soon as they see any mistakes, so have a colleague ready to note down all the comments.

For a large system, have efficient secretarial support ready to make changes the instant these are agreed. Hurrying the requirements along is necessary, even at the risk of making a few mistakes. Once users realize *they* have the right to fix the mistakes, they will soon sort out any problems.

Some users are happy with just a few words describing the purpose of each step. Others may need more explanation to relate each heading to their future tasks with the new system.

With a requirements tool or word-processor document viewed on screen, it is easy to attach audio-visual information such as graphs, diagrams or presentations, photos, and sound or video clips. Each item is played as you come to it: you can choose any order to illustrate different ways of using the system. Alternatively, simply make a presentation with one slide per scenario step.

Stepping through the scenarios makes them real

Begin the walkthrough by explaining what users will see: some simple examples of how their problem will be handled, how the future system will be used. Then walk through the steps you and the users have thought through. For example, to show how users would interact with a new system, you could show how the operator would start it up, select a particular option, run that option, hit a problem, fix the problem, and complete the job. This helps to create a realistic word picture, known as a use case, of part of a user's day.

You can even step through mock-up screens for a computer system, although the design of actual screens is usually best left until the requirements are completely defined. Apple Corporation designs its screens first, as a way of capturing the required user interactions for its software. This approach is controversial, but does have the merit of focussing attention on users, involving them in the design from the start.

Stepping through the required scenarios makes a future product 'real' for users, even if your images are simple, so expect plenty of feedback. Some users can get excited, especially if they feel you have forgotten their part of the problem.

Make clear the system is not designed yet

Especially if the show is on a computer screen, there is a danger that some users may think you have already designed and coded the system. Take care to explain that you have not made any design decisions, and that what the screen will show is just a concept. You will illustrate some possible sequences of events; the system as built will certainly look different.

Allow space for users to speak

Tell users they should feel free to interrupt at once if something is in the wrong place or missing. Introduce your colleague who is going to collect the feedback, and start the show. Explain what is happening as you go along, and keep an eye out for any user who wants to speak or ask a question. Agree any changes identified by users (Figure 8.1).

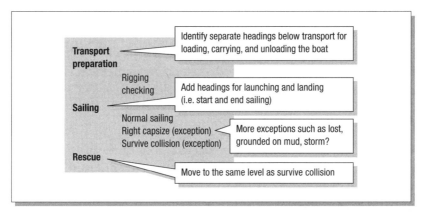

FIGURE 8.1 ■ Sailboat scenario structure annotated with feedback during a meeting

After the meeting – reorganize and reissue

After the meeting, tidy up and circulate the new version as soon as possible, and collect yet more feedback. This process is enjoyable for everyone, as they feel involved and progress is visible and quick.

8.2 Checking the requirements

Why checking matters

Checking is a cost-effective step

As far as we know, no system has ever started life with a complete and perfect set of requirements. Realistically, you must expect to draft, then review.

But drafting is error-prone, and formal review is time-consuming. Checking is a great way to find problems and save time, trouble, and money. This section suggests some simple checks that we have found to be effective. The same checks can be applied by reviewers as they prepare comments for a formal review.

What to check: individually and as a set

Requirements need to be checked individually, and most people if asked will look for and find weaknesses in individual statements. Each individual requirement must be clear, atomic, verifiable, prioritized, and have a known source.

But this, while helpful, is not sufficient. You also need to check the requirements as a set. The set as a whole must be realistic, consistent, and complete. This involves looking at the inter-relationships between requirements, and the totality of the set. Each requirement could seem sensible, but the total set could be impossible to implement.

Check each requirement

Check each requirement against this list. You'll find that quite soon you'll do this automatically whenever you see a requirement.

A list of simple checks

For each requirement, ask:

- Is it clear?
- Is it as short as it can be?
- Does it apply to a defined type of user?
- Does it have a reasonable priority?
- Is it verifiable?
- Is it a single requirement?
- Is its source shown?
- Does it have a unique identifier?
- Is it genuinely a user requirement, not a design constraint?

Examples of key points

The box opposite summarizes some of the key points for individual requirements.

A clear user requirement:

Type of user: The test engineer ...

Desired result: ... simulates ...

Object: ... the failure of any single component ...

Definite conditions: ... using only the built-in test facilities.

Attributes:

Identifier: **UR-75**

Importance: **Essential**

Review status: **Proposed**

Source: **M. Smith, Minutes M-38**

A vague expression of desirable features:

Vagueness?   In general, the system ...

Required or not?   ... should be able to ...

Which ones?   ... diagnose possible faults ...

How to verify that?   ... without requiring excessive downtime.

EXERCISE 16

Checking individual requirements

Here are some draft requirements which contain defects that might lead to difficulties later in the project. Identify the defects and improve the wording of each requirement accordingly.

Is it always possible to deduce the intended meaning of a defective requirement? If so, how? If not, what action should you take when you discover such a problem?

1   The driver shall be able to obtain instant action by giving any recognized voice command.

2   The operator shall be able to shut down the drive by disconnecting the power.

3 The extinguisher subsystem shall activate when the turbine temperature rises above the normal operating level.

4 In the unlikely event of an unexpected failure in the power train, the car shall stop without danger to the driver or passengers.

5 The mast-top radar reflector shall provide a bright radar return regardless of the orientation or attitude of the boat.

Check the requirements as a set

As well as checking individual requirements, it is necessary to check requirements as a set because they may interact with each other. This task is in general more difficult than checking a single requirement, as it is not sufficient to consider each paragraph or even each section on its own. Poorly structured requirements documents are very hard to check – a powerful argument in favor of taking the time to create a logical structure.

List of checks on requirement sets

To check the set of requirements as a whole, you need to know:

- Is it complete?
- Is it consistent?
- Is it realistic?
- Is it balanced, i.e. is each section covered in about the same amount of detail?

These are much tougher questions than those on individual requirements. The only way to answer them is for you and the users to have a clear picture in your minds of what the whole problem is, and for the user requirement structure to reflect that picture accurately.

Consistency and realism are tricky, too, because you have to think about what each requirement implies, and whether that is possible in the real world, given all the other requirements.

Can consistency be proved?

Consistency is a formal property which can, in principle, be proved in a formal specification. This offers the tempting vision of a way of writing requirements that are known to be correct. The problem is that there is no way to formalize a specification until the stakeholders agree what they want, and they won't understand the formalisms. What no theorem-prover can do is check whether a specification is what the stakeholders had in mind, or whether it has a realistic chance of being built. Therefore, we believe that user requirements should be written for humans to read and understand. Formal specification and proof may be useful in safety-critical system specifications, but they have little place in user requirements.

Some simple and useful checks can be automated. For example, every goal should be satisfied by at least one requirement. Later in a project, requirements tools can check that every user requirement is traced to at least one system specification, and to at least one acceptance test. These checks are valuable but do not guarantee completeness or consistency.

Keeping requirements documents short and checkable

Checking becomes close to impossible if the requirements document is too long for readers to keep in their heads. As Tony Hoare (Professor of Computing, University of Oxford) once remarked, there are two kinds of specifications: those where you can see that there aren't errors, and those where you can't see that there are errors. Make your requirements short and clear so that they can be checked easily. If there is any material that can be excluded, remove it.

EXERCISE 17

Checking a set of requirements

Here is a small set of requirements, each of which seems to make sense individually – but as a set there is something seriously wrong. The example may be a useful reminder that requirements do not always mean software.

1 *The sailboat shall be able to carry a crew of up to two adults and two 15-year-old children.*

2 *A crew of two adults or children shall be able to lift the sailboat on to its trailer.*

3 *The sailboat shall be controllable by a crew consisting of two persons aged between 7 and 70 in any wind between Force 1 and Force 6.*

a Identify what is wrong with this set of requirements.

b Redraft the requirement wording as far as you can.

c Identify what you would have to do to straighten out the requirements completely. (*Hint: who would you need to speak to?*)

d Write a change request explaining what you think should be done to improve the requirements as a set.

e Why does this kind of problem often arise?

f What would happen if these requirements were, respectively, on pages 3, 226, and 795 of the project documentation?

8.3 Reviewing

Checking can take place at any time and can be carried out by whoever is writing the requirements or by their colleagues. In contrast, reviews typically form project milestones, and take place at the end of project phases such as writing the user requirements. Reviews are always collaborative efforts. The techniques used to identify problems are the same as those used to check documents informally.

Reviews are meant to discover problems early enough to solve them quickly and cheaply. They start with careful preparation, so that comments are organized in time for the review meeting. The meeting itself makes decisions on all the review items. After the meeting, the review actions are chased until completed.

The review process

Main steps in a review cycle

Getting all stakeholders together in a meeting is expensive, so as much work as possible is done beforehand. The review process involves three main steps:

1 **Preparation:** obtaining review comments on a document from all stakeholders.

2 **Meeting:** deciding what to do about the comments, usually by agreeing changes to the requirements.

3 **Action:** making the agreed changes to the document.

Only the middle stage actually happens in the review meeting. The stakeholders themselves review the document in their own time before the meeting, writing comments and sending them in to the review organizer. The organizer has an intense job collecting and sorting all the comments to ensure the meeting runs smoothly.

Purpose of the meeting

The purpose of the meeting is to make decisions on the review suggestions, which are available in advance to everyone. The review aims to improve the quality of requirements. The idea is to focus the maximum amount of intelligence on to a document to define the problem as accurately as possible.

The job of editing the requirements document or taking any other action – such as finding out extra information – is done as soon as possible after the meeting.

Review – a process governed by requirements

Like many serious activities, reviewing needs to be treated as a game to get the best results. Different players have their own viewpoints and intentions which may be opposed by other players. This is why reviews must involve everybody with an interest in the problem, and why a 'games master' has to moderate the meetings. The debate on any point may be lively, but the time taken must be managed.

Users and developers have requirements on the review process itself, as if it was a product. There is an actual product: an agreed and baselined requirements document. A scenario structure for the review process is illustrated in Table 8.1.

TABLE 8.1 ■ Scenario structure for the review process

To review the requirements:
Prepare inputs
– Issue review plan
– Baseline working document
Obtain change requests
– Circulate working document
– Write change requests
Organize change requests
Decide on change requests (review meeting)
Dispose change requests
– Update working document
– Make agreed changes
– Issue new baseline
– Inform reviewers

First the requirements have to be frozen, so that everyone is "singing from the same songsheet." Keep an exact record of the version number and date of everything you send out to reviewers, with a reference copy in your project archive, and make a full backup of the review documents.

Some of the most common defects to look for in requirements are listed below. Notice that these are not just matters of how a single requirement is worded:

■ Design, methods and plans mixed in.

■ Solutions mixed with problems.

■ No clear owner.

■ No visible means of testing.

- Lack of structure: repetition, omissions.
- Ambiguity, vagueness, poor wording.
- Impractical set of requirements.

Reviewers can of course also apply any of the checks described in Section 8.2 while they are preparing formal review comments. For small informal developments, reviewers can write over identical printed copies of the document and send them back in. For bigger projects, it is better to suggest changes on a specific form. The review manager collects all the suggestions, and sorts them into the order of the document. Where several people have made the same point, the suggestions are literally or figuratively stapled together so that they are handled as one.

In the review meeting, step through the suggestions, deciding whether to accept or reject them. The same principles of running a co-operative meeting apply as in workshops with stakeholders (see Section 3.3). Document all the meeting's decisions as you go along. If more work is needed before a decision can be reached, allocate some time after the review meeting for that work.

After the meeting, step through all the decisions of the review and produce an updated version of the requirements document.

Guidelines for reviewing

Build a team of skilled reviewers

You'll find that a few specific people make the best reviewers, time and again. Cultivate them and make sure they have time allocated for the work.

Encourage criticism

Encourage criticism – remember that people are improving the requirements, not criticizing you. Even the most vitriolic criticism often contains a grain of truth.

Chase all the corrections

The review isn't finished until all the corrections have been made and agreed. Allocate the available time sensibly so that you cover all suggestions. Allow only three decision outcomes – accept, reject, and accept with modifications. Keep up the pace of decision-making. Be firm: you don't have to be nice to be a good reviewer.

Make documents short and simple

To review any individual requirement in a document, people have to understand its relationships to other requirements. Strive to minimize the number of inter-relationships by providing a logical structure.

Review informally until you're sure of success first time

Aim to get everything right in a single formal review. Small-scale, informal reviews and inspections with your colleagues can happen any time. Continue with these until you are sure that passing the formal review will be just a formality.

8.4 Success – the reviewed document

Once the agreed changes have been put into the requirements, the document should be baselined and a copy placed in the project library. You now have a set of requirements which, if not perfect, does at least represent the combined knowledge and wishes of the whole team. Your project is off to an excellent start.

EXERCISE 18

Reviewing

Identify the faults in the following requirements (after the example):

The refrigerator shall have a user-controllable setting for the amount of cooling to be applied.

Defects:

- This is a system specification, not a user requirement.

- The user wants to control the temperature not cooling effort.

- The user's real need is for safe food.

■ Safety limits need to be specified and checked.

■ The user must be warned if there is danger.

The driver shall be able to lock the differentials to optimize performance and driving pleasure during off-road driving.

Defects:

■

■

■

A backup of all customer account data shall be made every night between 9PM and 6AM.

Defects:

■

■

■

Summary

This book describes writing requirements as part of a process of dialog and negotiation between requirements engineers and stakeholders. We do not think that writing can be treated as a stand-alone activity; instead, requirements must bridge the gap between the people who have a problem that a system might solve, and the people who can build such a system. The scope of the book is set to cover only the user requirements, i.e. the problem description; system and subsystem specification is not discussed here in any detail, although some of the techniques discussed can be applied to specifications.

The requirements process begins by identifying the stakeholders who need to be involved in the process. Next is a complex set of activities, gathering requirements. Requirements can come from many possible sources, which we divide into people and products. The people who can contribute requirements are by definition the stakeholders; effective techniques for gathering requirements from them include interviewing and workshops of various kinds. A wide range of other sources include existing products, whether these are older models or rival offerings, problem reports, customer suggestions, and prototypes. Requirements from any of these sources must be checked with stakeholders.

Perhaps the key to the whole process is an effective way of organizing the requirements. We believe that it is best to follow the way the users see their own problem. This means that each part of the problem is described in the order in which users would encounter it. The requirements are grouped under headings, each of which is the name of a goal; the highest-level goal is the problem that the system will have to solve. An immediate effect of this organization is that a sequence of headings can be read as a simple scenario: the users do this, then they do that. This structure constantly provides the reader with the context for each subgoal and each requirement, removing much of the ambiguity and confusion that dogs many attempts at writing requirements.

The requirements are further set in context by providing whatever subsidiary information may be needed. Rather than imagining each requirement as a piece of text, swimming by itself in a sea of print, it is treated as an engineering component, suitably bagged and labeled with attributes describing its status, and linked to other components such as specifications and test steps.

The task of actually writing the requirement text, given that we already know who owns the requirement, how important it is, what goal it serves, and so on, is reduced to the relatively simple task of stating in a single sentence who wants what to happen, and in what way. Since the text does not have to do all the work, natural language can be exploited to provide a simple, clear communication of intention.

No attempt at describing a problem is exactly right first time. We describe a range of simple checks and standard techniques to refine and review the requirements.

Finally, the book is intended to be a practical introduction to the field for students and new practitioners. Each chapter contains simple exercises illustrating its key points, with hints and suggested answers.

Appendix

Example user requirements for a burglar alarm

This small example illustrates one way of organizing and writing requirements, namely as nested scenarios. We hope you find the example informative. It is not perfect; you may like to practice your reviewing skills on it (see Chapter 8). However, we think it is simple and clear.

Note that some requirements are listed even though they are not approved. This marks them as issues that are being or have already been considered. If you are using a database to hold your requirements, you can choose to print out only the approved requirements.

Reading the requirements

- Cross-references to included scenarios are <u>underlined</u>.

- The primary user for a scenario is shown in **boldface**. The stated users apply to all the steps in a scenario.

- Exception events are named at the start of their requirements, followed by a colon, e.g. "Alarm Not Activated:".

- Steps that simply record external events to set the scene are shown with void priority and status, like this: ---.

ID	Requirements (structured as scenarios)	Users	Priority	Status
UR-3	**2.1 Use burglar alarm**			
UR-30	**2.1.1 Protect the house**	**Householder**		
UR-32	**2.1.1.1 Primary scenario**			
UR-31	Householder uses an alarm to protect the house on each <u>normal day</u>.		Essential	Approved
UR-405	Maintenance engineer routinely <u>services the alarm</u> once a year.		Essential	Approved
UR-34	**2.1.1.2 Exceptions**			
UR-38	Alarm not activated: sound buzzer to warn householder.		Possibly useful	Rejected
UR-5	**2.1.2 Normal day**	**Householder**		
UR-40	**2.1.2.1 Primary scenario**			
UR-7	Householder activates alarm; alarm sounds buzzer.		Essential	Approved
UR-8	Householder closes door; alarm stops sounding buzzer.		Essential	Approved
UR-29	Alarm listens out on all its sensors for possible <u>detected intrusion</u>.		Essential	Approved
UR-9	Householder opens door; alarm sounds buzzer.		Essential	Approved
UR-10	Householder deactivates alarm.		Essential	Approved
UR-183	**2.1.3 Detected intrusion**			
UR-184	**2.1.3.1 Primary scenario**			
UR-188	Alarm detects signs such as movement in the house.		Essential	Approved
UR-192	Alarm identifies possible attempt to <u>burgle the house</u>.		Essential	Approved
UR-193	Alarm notifies the call center of possible intrusion.		Essential	Approved
UR-194	Call center <u>handles possible intrusion</u>.		Essential	Approved
UR-186	**2.1.3.2 Exceptions**			
UR-190	Power cut: <u>run without power</u>.		Essential	Approved
UR-693	Signals cut: alarm signals to call center without using wires.		Desirable	On hold
UR-195	**2.1.4 Handle possible intrusion**	**Call center operator** Guard		
UR-196	**2.1.4.1 Primary scenario**			
UR-200	Call center operator views details of reported intrusion.		Essential	Approved

ID	Requirements (structured as scenarios)	Users	Priority	Status
UR-204	Call center operator tries to disconfirm intrusion by calling householder.		Essential	Approved
UR-205	Call center operator calls out guard.		Essential	Approved
UR-198	**2.1.4.2 Exceptions**			
UR-202	Mistake by householder: call center logs event and does not call out guard.		Essential	Approved
UR-320	Transient false alarm: call center logs event and does not call out guard.		Essential	Approved
UR-655	**2.1.5 Run without power**			
UR-656	**2.1.5.1 Primary scenario**			
UR-660	Alarm runs on battery power for at least 12 hours.		Essential	Approved
UR-664	**2.1.5.2 Trigger**			
UR-665	Mains power fails.		---	---
UR-182	**2.2 Handle problems**			
UR-128	**2.2.1 Alarm breakdown**	Call center operator		
UR-129	**2.2.1.1 Primary scenario**			
UR-133	Alarm fails.		---	---
UR-146	Alarm notifies failure to call center.		Essential	Approved
UR-161	Call center operator arranges to repair failed alarm.		Essential	Approved
UR-131	**2.2.1.2 Exceptions**			
UR-158	Alarm unable to notify failure: TBD		Desirable	Draft
UR-160	Communications broken: TBD		Desirable	Draft
UR-406	**2.2.2 Service the alarm**	Householder Call center operator **Maintenance engineer**		
UR-407	**2.2.2.1 Primary scenario**			
UR-411	Call center operator arranges an appointment with the householder.		Essential	Approved
UR-425	Call center operator schedules a maintenance engineer to service the alarm on the agreed date.		Essential	Approved
UR-426	Maintenance engineer reads the schedule on the agreed date, and travels to the householder's address.		Essential	Approved
UR-427	Maintenance engineer runs the standard diagnostic checks on the alarm.		Essential	Approved

ID	Requirements (structured as scenarios)	Users	Priority	Status
UR-408	**2.2.2.2 Alternative paths**			
UR-412	**2.2.2.2.1 Householder changes time of appointment**			
UR-788	Householder contacts call center operator to change the appointment.		Essential	Approved
UR-789	Call center operator updates the maintenance schedule.		Essential	Approved
UR-409	**2.2.2.3 Exceptions**			
UR-413	Alarm is faulty: maintenance engineer repairs failed alarm and tests it again to ensure it is working correctly.		Essential	Approved
UR-428	Alarm irreparable: maintenance engineer logs the problem, informs the householder that the alarm needs to be replaced, and makes an appointment with the householder for a return visit. The same maintenance engineer returns on the agreed date to replace the alarm.		Essential	Approved
UR-410	**2.2.2.4 Constraints**			
UR-414	One-star service contract holders are not guaranteed their choice of service date.		Essential	Approved
UR-415	**2.2.2.5 Trigger**			
UR-416	A year has elapsed since installation or the last service.		Essential	Approved
UR-417	**2.2.2.6 Preconditions**			
UR-418	Householder has a valid maintenance contract with the alarm company.		Essential	Approved
UR-271	**2.2.3 Repair failed alarm**	**Maintenance engineer**		
UR-272	**2.2.3.1 Primary scenario**			
UR-276	Maintenance engineer examines alarm's self-test diagnostics.		Essential	Approved
UR-342	Maintenance engineer replaces failed components.		Essential	Approved
UR-343	Maintenance engineer tests the alarm.		Essential	Approved
UR-273	**2.2.3.2 Alternative paths**			
UR-277	Maintenance engineer orders a component not held in stock from its supplier, agrees a suitable date for a second visit, and asks call center operator to schedule the second visit appointment.		Essential	Approved

ID	Requirements (structured as scenarios)	Users	Priority	Status
UR-344	Call center operator schedules the second visit.		Essential	Approved
UR-345	Maintenance engineer replaces the non-stock component and tests the alarm.		Essential	Approved
UR-137	**2.2.4 Power failure**	Call center operator		
UR-138	**2.2.4.1 Primary scenario**			
UR-340	Alarm notifies power failure to call center.		Essential	Approved
UR-142	Alarm's batteries allow the alarm to <u>run without power</u> normally for 24 hours.		Essential	Approved
UR-143	When power is restored, alarm recharges battery and notifies end of power failure incident to call center.		Essential	Approved
UR-139	**2.2.4.2 Alternative paths**			
UR-346	Alarm notifies impending battery exhaustion to call center.		Desirable	On hold
UR-140	**2.2.4.3 Exceptions**			
UR-144	Batteries fail early: call center operator contacts householder and arranges to <u>repair failed alarm</u>.		Possibly useful	On hold
UR-700	**3 Non-functional requirements**			
UR-701	**3.1 Market**			
UR-702	The five-room version of the household alarm has a retail price of no more than US$1,000.		Essential	Approved
UR-703	**3.2 Reliability**			
UR-704	The household alarm fails so as to require repair no more than once every ten years on average.		Essential	Approved
UR-705	The call center fails so as to require repair no more than once every year on average.		Essential	Approved
UR-706	**3.3 Safety**			
UR-707	The household alarm is electrically safe for household use.		Essential	Approved
UR-708	The call center is electrically safe for commercial office use.		Essential	Approved

ID	Requirements (structured as scenarios)	Users	Priority	Status
UR-709	**3.4 Usability**			
UR-710	The household alarm can be used correctly by 95% of householders after five minutes of instruction.		Essential	Approved
UR-711	The household alarm can be diagnosed, repaired, and tested correctly by 95% of maintenance engineers after two weeks of instruction.		Essential	Approved
UR-712	The call center can be operated correctly by 95% of operators after one week of instruction.		Essential	Approved
UR-713	**3.4 Environment**			
UR-714	The household alarm's outdoor components are sufficiently waterproof and corrosion-resistant to remain in working order for ten years.		Essential	Approved

Answers to exercises

We have tried in the following answers to provide some analysis of the set problems. We hope the exercises are reasonably self-contained, but inevitably other answers are possible. In places we have provided suggestions for more extended answers.

Exercise 1 Listing the stakeholders

Truck driver; Controller; Mechanic

Jack Schmidt – senior driver;

Bill Higgins – assistant driver;

Jane Sikorsky – controller;

Mike Olausson – mechanic.

Exercise 2 Asking "why?"

1 The coffee pot.

I want hot fresh coffee whenever I walk into the kitchen.

I want to be able to make coffee without risking injury or damage.

Obviously these are only sketches as written. More practical requirements, using the shorthand "cook" for the person who wants to make coffee, might be:

The cook makes hot coffee within a few minutes, putting ground coffee and cold water into the coffee-maker.

The cook safely operates the coffee-maker in an office kitchen with wet hands.

2   The bottle-warmer.

Existing design: The bottle-warmer displays a red light when the power is applied, but the light goes out when the specified temperature is reached.

It is not stated why it behaves like this, but the underlying requirements are probably:

The cook can see when the bottle-warmer is connected to a live electricity supply.

The cook can select a desired temperature for the bottle.

The cook can see when the bottle has reached the specified temperature.

It is notable that the original statement implied a single lamp, unable to meet the underlying requirements properly except by tricks such as making it flash, thus giving it two outputs – steady and flashing – to convey the two required active states. Presumably this was driven by cost. A yellow light for power, and a green light for temperature reached, would be better.

Exercise 3 Extracting requirements from source documents

Classify the statements (a) to (n):

1   user requirements: (b) (c) (e) (g) (h) (j) (and possibly part of d)

2   system specifications: (i)

3   design elements: (f) (n)

4   plans: (k) (l) (m)

5   background material: (a)

6   irrelevant detail: (d)

Note: Delivery schedule dates are close to being user requirements. In the extreme case, a space mission to rendezvous with a comet (such as spacecraft Giotto's exploration of Halley's Comet) is now or never: the launch date is certainly a requirement. But schedules often change even when the requirements are essentially stable, so as a rule, don't put dates into the requirements.

Exercise 4 Extracting requirements from a memo

Here is a small subset of the requirements suggested by the memo.

New product: *small family sailboat.*

Marketing constraints

Sailboat is attractively packaged.

Sailboat is marketed to be fun for all the family to sail on lake, river, or coastal water.

Sailboat is marketed as safe.

Sailboat is marketed as easy to handle.

Its target price is $TBD.

Sailing

Sailboat carries two crew, aged 7 to 70.

Crew can sail on fresh water.

Crew can sail on salt water.

Crew can control boat in a light to moderately strong wind.

Capsize

Crew can right capsized boat from any attitude in the water.

Safety

Sailboat floats when capsized.

Sailboat floats when holed.

Crew can attract rescue.

Transport

Sailboat is sized to fit readily in the home's garage.

Sailboat is towed behind a compact family car.

Towed sailboat complies with road traffic regulations.

You could also consider scenarios – each with a separate section – for manufacturing, maintenance, and disposal. Notice that these are part of a large-scale, whole-life cycle scenario for a sailboat: make, sell, sail, transport, store, maintain, dispose. Have you thought about the equivalent scenarios for your systems?

Exercise 5 A structure for user requirements

This exercise can be done in as much detail as desired, up to a self-taught project covering a complete set of requirements. Here is one goal in full.

Overall goal: *To maintain customers' [gas] installations.*

Goal 1: To receive service request from existing customer (actor: call center operator)

Step 1: [To] Answer telephone

Step 2: [To] Identify customer

Step 3: [To] Identify service needed

Step 4: [To] Identify available appointment times

Step 5: [To] Agree appointment

Step 6: [To] Record the order

Goal 2: To service the installation (actor: maintenance engineer)

Step 1: [To] Read appointment details

Step 2: [To] Plan route

Step 3: [To] Drive to customer's site

Step 4: [To] …

Exercise 6 Could anything go wrong here?

This is an exercise with many possible answers. For example:

To select a radio channel

The truck driver shall be able to select a radio channel by spoken command.

(exception) The driver selects a channel by accident.

(steps to take) Select the right channel again, or use a "go back" command.

(other exceptions) Driver could also switch off the radio by accident.

(prevention) Learn to avoid the command words in radio dialog; commands could require confirmation, or be prefixed by words not used normally.

To prepare the sailboat for sailing

A crew of two persons aged at least seven years shall be able to prepare the sailboat for sailing within ten minutes.

Sailboat is rigged unsafely.

Check rigging for dangers, fix detected problems, check again.

Mast could be loose, steering unpinned.

Training course; checklist built into sailboat; parts lock audibly into position.

To drive on an icy surface

The driver shall be able to control the car on an icy surface at any speed up to 20 kilometers per hour.

Wheels spin on slippery surface.

Reduce power, stop braking, turn wheel in opposite direction.

Car could spin or turn over.

Lockable differentials; auto-detect slipping; anti-lock brakes. (*Note that these are all possible solutions; they could be handled as system specifications or as design decisions, but are not user requirements.*)

To detect intrusion

The alarm shall sound within 30 seconds when an attempt is made to enter the protected house.

Householder enters house and sets off alarm.

Switch off alarm; notify call center.

Wind, insects, animals, postmen set off alarm.

Discriminate non-intrusive disturbances; require evidence of actual intrusion; allow more time for householder to disable alarm.

Exercise 7 Exceptions

a   Try to list all the exceptions that could arise when a plane lands.

There are many, including:

- a tire bursts;
- a tire catches fire on braking;
- a thrust reverser fails to operate;
- the plane is too high on approach;
- fog covers the runway;
- the plane is running out of fuel;
- ...

b   Write user requirements to cover all your exceptions.

The requirements need to ask for safe handling of each case. For example:

- The plane lands safely in the event of a burst in any single tire.
- The plane stops safely in the event of fire in any number of its tires.
- ...

Your own system: you can expect to find at least one plausible exception for every user goal. Use the guidelines in this book to check your user requirements on these exceptions.

For example, in an e-commerce system, the customer may fill in any of the fields incorrectly, or leave them blank. The system may be able to catch some of these errors by validating the data and cross-checking, e.g. the zip code can be checked against the city. The internet connection may be lost. The orders database or its server may crash.

Exercise 8 Creating a heading structure

The example in the text is fine as far as it goes, but is only a first attempt: expect to revise requirements a few times. Other areas that ought to be covered include:

- Plan the flight.
- Obtain weather forecast.
- Estimate passengers and cargo.

- Select best route.
- Calculate fuel.
- Prepare flight plan.
- Submit flight plan to air traffic control.
- Plan the flight schedules.
- ...
- Plan the maintenance.
- ...
- Plan the staff rota.
- ...
- Plan the pricing structure.
- ...
- ...

Note that there is often far more behind-the-scenes work to be thought about than appears to the customer or passenger.

Exercise 9 The right document for each subject

There is not enough information simply in the headings to make it possible to guess what each section might contain. Probably all the sections contain a mixture of requirements and design. However, a preliminary allocation might be:

User requirements	4.2, 4.3 (perhaps), 5.4
System specifications	3.1, 4.1, 4.3 (perhaps), 5.2, 5.3
System design	4.5
Development plan	3.2, 3.3, 4.4
Maintenance plan	5.1
Unknown	5.5, 5.6

Exercise 10 Wrongly placed requirements

A possible allocation to sections is:

Preparation for flight   (d)

Takeoff and landing   (e) (f) (g)

Flight   (c)*

Maintenance   (h)

Safety   (c)*

Performance   (b)

Materials   (a) (i)

* Some of the requirements could be treated in more than one section – safety of a material could be section 5 or 7, safety in flight could be 3 or 5, and so on. This suggests that the proposed list of sections is not ideal as it stands. It might be better to separate constraints that apply to just one activity, such as flight safety or ground safety, from general constraints that apply throughout, such as materials.

Materials requirements would be better placed in the aircraft (system) specification rather than here; the underlying user requirement is simply for safety.

Exercise 11 Writing constraints

■ Define the levels of dependability users require of a system you are familiar with, or of the trucker's mobile communications system in the example project.

It might be possible to write a single user requirement for dependability:

The driver loses contact with control for no more than 30 minutes on any journey in the states served by the system.

In other systems, you may need to think out a set of related dependability requirements. For instance, in an office computer network, the file server and backup mechanisms must be highly dependable, but individual workstations can be less so, allowing for important cost savings.

- Safety constraints for the people cleaning the windows of a 100-story building.

  Our first attempt might be:

  The window-cleaners are able to work safely…

  but on reflection it is clear that this is only possible:

  …within the approved limits of weather.

  It is then necessary to define such limits. This seems more like a set of system specifications than user requirements:

  Approved limits of weather:

  Temperature 5 to 30 °C.

  Wind force 0 to 4 Beaufort.

  Rain up to 5 mm per hour.

  Daylight.

  If we accept this approach, the 'escape' requirement is:

  The window-cleaners are able to return to a safe place when weather conditions depart from the approved limits.

  The ultimate requirement might be simply that the workers are always safe: whether they can work or not in certain conditions is arguably a matter for the design of the system. Unfortunately, this is a bit vague. As often happens, there is no perfect answer to the division of responsibility between requirements and design, but it is certainly better to think such arguments through at the user requirements stage.

- Performance constraints for the window-cleaners of a 100-story building.

  The window-cleaners are able to travel to any chosen window on any story within five minutes from any position of the cleaning platform.

Exercise 12 Restricting the scope

Original requirement	Restricted requirement	Why was it restricted?
The window-cleaners shall be able to work at any time...	... in the approved weather conditions.	Because working in extreme heat, cold, rain, or wind is unsafe given feasible assumptions about design.
Truckers shall be able to communicate instantly with their controllers from any location on their routes...	... within 15 seconds ... within 50 miles of any major city ...	Because the controllers may be busy with other calls. Because affordable connection depends on existing provision by telephone utilities.

Exercise 13 Good requirements

"The communication system shall break down no more than twice per year."

We can't legislate for how often it will fail, but can require it to be available 363 days per year, for example. There may also be a need for requirements on what it does when overloaded: to carry traffic at 100% of normal loading and delay the rest, for example.

"The system shall be easy to use by personnel with minimal training."

Unverifiable, not a requirement. Easy in what way? By whom? What sort of training? Which part of the system? A better approach is to break down the training requirements according to user type and task. For example,

"Operators shall be able to make a full backup after one day's training."

"The average delay to the user caused by the motorway toll system shall be less than 15 seconds."

Presumably the "user" is a driver in this case. What is a delay? How is it defined? The term may well be defined separately in the requirements document so that it can be referred to in several requirements. It might be "increase in journey time," for example.

Can truck drivers be handled as rapidly as car drivers? It would be better to write *"The average delay to the car driver ..."*

"All users shall use the same commercial software for project management."

What they use is a matter for staff discipline. The company can provide a standard package to all project managers. It is unlikely that other "users" will need the package at all. So: *"All project managers shall have access to the standard project management package."*

But perhaps the real issue is why the project managers should have the same software. The reasons (requirements) might be:

- to minimize training and support costs;

- to obtain bulk purchase discounts;

- to enable information to be shared.

As usual, asking "why?" leads to better requirements.

"The maximum delay between transmission and reception of an invoice shall be two hours."

Reception where? By whom? Why? Perhaps: *"Finance shall be able to read each invoice within two hours of its issue by Accounts."* This constraint shows that performance requirements can link a pair of functions: in this case, to transmit and to receive an invoice.

"The database shall store ten years of records."

Storing is not a user requirement – retrieving is. To be verifiable, this requires estimates of projected data volumes. What the users presumably need to do is to be able to evaluate and compare (and so on) historical records up to ten years old. There may be several user requirements here, but the requirement as stated gives little clue as to what these might be.

"The call dispatcher shall be able to communicate by radio to the ambulance driver."

Needs acceptance criteria for performance, e.g. "within ten seconds." "By radio" is arguably a solution and forms part of the design; it is at least a system specification. The user requirement is simply to be able to communicate whatever the ambulance is doing.

Exercise 14 Writing requirements for familiar domestic systems

Refrigerator

Example answers are given in the exercise text. A possible addition is:

The cook takes the food from the refrigerator at a temperature that allows immediate eating or cooking (i.e. not frozen).

Toaster

Sketch of requirement: *Cook gets pieces of bread of any reasonable size, shape, and consistency toasted until brown, crunchy, and hot, within a few minutes, without danger.*

This probably needs to be analyzed into several requirement statements. Notice that it is often easy to describe the overall intention, even if it is difficult to be precise about it. Such a rough sketch of intention is a valuable piece of requirements documentation, as it helps readers to understand what is really wanted, and allows analysts to validate the requirements.

Burglar alarm

Sketch of requirement: *Householder sets alarm when leaving house and unsets it when returning. While householder is out, alarm protects house, calling a guard whenever an intrusion occurs and at no other time.*

This goal is in practice difficult to achieve. Notice that the sketch turns naturally into scenarios.

Exercise 15 Ambiguous requirements

Try to work out what the authors of these two requirements must have intended, and redraft these intentions as user requirements.

It isn't possible to tell. If you split each sentence so that there are no "and"s left you get several statements that might become requirements, but which conflict with each other.

What additional information would you need to make good requirements in these cases? You need to discover the intentions of the users in each case. Where the users are not identified, you need to discover who they are and proceed from there.

Who would you need to consult? You will need to consult with management as well as users, to ensure that sufficient resources are made available to you to complete the requirements adequately.

Exercise 16 Checking individual requirements

Defects

1 *The driver shall be able to obtain instant action by giving any recognized voice command.*

Instantly is wishful thinking. A timespan is needed. What about possible misrecognition? Do some commands need confirmation rather than instant response?

2 *The operator shall be able to shut down the drive by disconnecting the power.*

The drive will probably shut down anyway if the power goes, but in what state? Probably, data needs to be saved; moving parts may need to be stowed safely; alarms and indicators may need to be activated or suppressed. We need to find out who stated the requirement, and then discuss with them what they actually need. It might be something like

"The operator is able to shut down the drive safely in a single operation taking no more than five seconds"

but we can't tell without talking to the user.

3 *The extinguisher subsystem shall activate when the turbine temperature rises above the normal operating level.*

How much above? A threshold is needed. What is normal? This is a (sub)system specification, not a user requirement. The underlying requirement is to prevent fire from spreading.

4 *In the unlikely event of an unexpected failure in the power train, the car shall stop without danger to the driver or passengers.*

The first half of this is publicity, not requirement. It is worded as a vague system specification; the user requirement should begin with "The driver shall be able to stop the car … ."

Danger can be expected in such a situation. The underlying requirement is presumably "…with control, despite failure of the power train."

5 *The mast-top radar reflector shall provide a bright radar return regardless of the orientation or attitude of the boat.*

This is going to be difficult if the mast-top is under water. What the users may have wanted to say is:

Sketch of requirement: *The coastguard shall be able to see the sailboat easily by radar, whatever the boat is doing.*

This requirement needs to be sharpened up in discussions with the coastguard. There might also be a matching requirement for ships to see the sailboat.

Is it always possible to deduce the intended meaning of a defective requirement?

No, as the examples above illustrate.

What action should you take when you discover such a problem?

i   Mark the requirement as not ready for review.

ii Identify the owner of the requirement.

iii Discuss with them the intention of the requirement.

iv Redraft the wording.

v   Mark the requirement as ready for review.

Exercise 17 Checking a set of requirements

The sailboat shall be able to carry a crew of up to two adults and two 15-year-old children.

A crew of two adults or children shall be able to lift the sailboat on to its trailer.

The sailboat shall be controllable by a crew consisting of two persons aged between 7 and 70 in any wind between Force 1 and Force 6.

The number and age composition of crew is not consistently defined. It would be best defined just once; other requirements can then safely refer to "the crew…" as a user class. Incidentally, two of these are written as sailboat specifications, not as user requirements. The use of the conjunctions "and" and "or" in the individual requirements does not seem especially dangerous here, but is perhaps best avoided.

- The crew shall consist of two persons aged between 7 and 70.

- The crew shall be able to sail on fresh water.

- The crew shall be able to sail on salt water.

Carrying capacity depends on buoyancy, which depends on the type of water; but also, the safety requirements for sailing on the sea are more severe. This requirement is tricky as it requires the reader to look up the definition of crew, and the writer to know about buoyancy. Trickiness suggests that more analysis and explanation is needed. In this case the headings "carrying capacity" and "buoyancy" would help.

The crew shall be able to lift the sailboat …

The crew shall be able to control the sailboat …

Marketing will have to decide how many crew are to be carried. This has strong effects on the handling and liveliness of the sailboat, and on the price. See the comments above on the size and age of the crew. You need to explain what the problem is, why it matters, and what might be done about it. In this case the priority is high, as the composition of the crew is crucial for the design.

Consider different market sectors or stakeholders. The young family with an adventurous father needs quite a different sailboat from the teenagers out for excitement.

The problems would surface during design, or if not, during acceptance testing, at which point they would be costly to fix. If testing was as skimpy as requirements handling, the market would give its own final answer.

Exercise 18 Reviewing

The driver shall be able to lock the differentials to optimize performance and driving pleasure during off-road driving.

Defects:

- Talk of optimizing pleasure is publicity material, not requirements.

- The user requirement is to drive safely on a slippery surface; the lockable differential is a subsystem which may or may not be provided in the chosen design; the need might be met better by other possible solutions.

A backup of all customer account data shall be made every night between 9PM and 6AM.

Defects:

- Why in the night? The unstated requirement here is presumably to have the data backed up without interfering with customer service. If operations become global, when is the night?

- Why a backup? The need is to be able to restore full service in the event of a crash of some kind. A backup is one type of solution; a hot standby is another. Nobody ever wants to save data; people want to be able to read it and use it regardless of interruptions.

Glossary

Cross-references to other glossary entries are in **boldface**.

Acceptance criterion
Precisely defined condition that a **system** must meet in order to be accepted; a component of a **requirement**.

Affordance
A **requirement** that affords an option or freedom to a **user**, whether or not the **user** chooses to exploit it.

Capability
In a **system specification**, a function that a system is capable of but performs only when requested to by a user or another system. **Functions** not exposed to agents outside the system are not capabilities. However, the term is often used loosely to mean no more than "system function." In **user requirements**, a capability means something a user wants to be able to do, so in this sense it is a synonym for **affordance**.

Constraint
A statement of restriction, modifying a requirement or set of requirements by limiting the range of acceptable solutions. Sometimes used to indicate physical limitations such as on size, shape, weight. Constraints may be imposed either by **users** (in **user requirements**) or by **developers** with specialist knowledge, such as of safety standards (in **system requirements**).

Customer
A person who pays for a system development, including the requirements. *Compare*: **user, stakeholder**.

Design constraint
Constraint describing an existing interface, presumably part of the design of some existing or legacy system that must be complied with.

Developer	A person who is involved in developing a system to satisfy the **user requirements**.
Exception (event)	Undesired event from any source, threatening a desired system **goal**. Exception events need to be handled by appropriate **exception scenarios**.
Exception scenario	The desired response (sequence of actions) to an exception event. It results in an end-state which is safe, and which is, if possible, back at some step in a normal scenario, so that users can continue with their work. In other words, the goal for an exception scenario is to handle the **exception event** safely.
Fit criterion	*See* **acceptance criterion**.
Function	Something that a system or subsystem does, presumably because a **requirement** made it necessary.
Functional requirement	A **requirement** for a **function**. *Compare*: **NFR**.
Goal	A desired result, often at a high and abstract level. Goals are useful as the names of **scenarios** or **use cases** used to structure **requirements**.
Inquiry cycle	A structured sequence of activities, designed to be repeated as necessary, often in a **workshop**, to achieve consensus among a group of **stakeholders**, e.g. on a set of **requirements**.
NFR	*See* **non-functional requirement**.
Non-functional requirement	= **constraint**; any **requirement** other than a **function**. **NFR**s that do not refer to physical attributes like weight are also called 'qualities' or simply '-ilities.'
Operator	A **user** who is responsible for operating a **system**, e.g. controlling it from a console.
Priority	1) The (input) value attached to a requirement by a **stakeholder**. 2) The (output) agreed relative importance of a requirement compared to the other requirements in a document or set.

Prototype   A mock-up, working model, presentation, or other device giving the appearance of or supplying some part of the behavior of the **system**, so as to assist **stakeholders** in defining their **requirements**.

Requirement   1) A **user requirement**. 2) A **system requirement**.

Requirements engineer   A person who helps to formulate user and system requirements.

Review   The formal, structured process in which **stakeholders** and **developers** check that a requirements document is satisfactory and agree changes. Its central component is a meeting, but this is preceded and followed by numerous essential activities.

Scenario   A time-ordered sequence of activities used to structure a set of **requirements** according to their actual or predicted pattern of usage.

Scope   Whatever (requirements) the system is to cover. Often implemented by maintaining an in/out attribute list to show which requirement is to be satisfied by which version of a **system**.

Specification   The precise definition of the required behavior and qualities of a **system** in a form suitable for inclusion in a contract.

Stakeholder   A person who has a legitimate interest in a **system** and can therefore state **requirements**.

System   The **system** under design, the combination of hardware and software that is to be developed to satisfy the **requirements**.

System function   *See* **function**.

System requirement   Either an **affordance** or a **constraint**, forming a structured element of a **system specification**.

System specification   A **specification** for a **system**.

Traceability The management of traces between engineering objects such as requirements, tests, and design elements, e.g. with a requirements database. Its purpose is to enable **verification** and **validation** by showing that requirements are met, and to enable rational choices if time or money run short by relating cuts in design or test to the priorities of the associated requirements.

Use case Structured format, such as the one proposed by Alistair Cockburn, for organizing a set of closely related scenarios (describing normal, alternative, and exception sequences) and associated conditions into a compact and readable unit a few pages in length.

User 1) *(strict sense)* A **stakeholder** who directly uses (or will directly use) the **system**. 2) *(loose sense)* A **stakeholder** closely involved in a development project.

User requirement A structured statement of **user** or other **stakeholder** need (in the world), written as either an **affordance** or as a **constraint**, imposed by a user. *Compare*: **system requirement**.

Validation Checking that the **requirements** as documented are indeed the right ones, namely the ones that the **stakeholders** actually want. *Compare*: **verification**.

Verification Demonstrating that: 1) a **system** meets its **system specification**; 2) a **system** in use meets its **user requirements**. Verification is most often by test but can also be by inspection, analysis, or simulation. *Compare*: **validation**.

Viewpoint (A statement of) the point of view of a **stakeholder**.

Workshop An interactive, facilitated meeting of **stakeholders** organized to capture and validate **user requirements**.

Further reading

This list of books is meant to be a practical starting point for readers who wish to learn more than the brief summary of requirements engineering given in this book. As far as possible, we have chosen books that are widely available; we have listed papers only when we knew no textbook that covered the topic in question.

The books listed here, and others on related topics, are reviewed in detail on a website maintained by one of us (Alexander) at
http://easyweb.easynet.co.uk/~iany/reviews/reviews.htm

Requirements expression

There are few books that cover the actual writing and expression of requirements, and some of those that do are not especially helpful. A recent book that is well written, entertaining, often controversial, possibly weak on structuring requirements, but well worth dipping into, is

Practical Software Requirements, A manual of content and style, Ben Kovitz, Manning, 1999 (ISBN 1-884777-59-7).

Requirements engineering

A useful and practical textbook from experienced practitioners, advocating a fully worked-out and very detailed method and template (VOLERE) for engineering requirements, is

Mastering the Requirements Process, Suzanne Robertson and James Robertson, ACM Press, Addison-Wesley, 1999 (ISBN 0-201-36046-2).

A more academic but still useful textbook, rather weak on scenarios and requirements organization but offering much help and advice on elicitation, validation, and viewpoints is

Requirements Engineering, processes and techniques, Gerald Kotonya and Ian Sommerville, John Wiley & Sons, 1997 (ISBN 0-471-97208-8).

A source of ideas for techniques that you may want to try out or evaluate for possible use is given in the following book. It is divided into "guidelines," most of which take up two or three pages, with cross-references. There are few examples and the recommendations are treated separately, so the advice may be difficult to translate into project practice.

Requirements Engineering: A good practice guide, Ian Sommerville and Pete Sawyer, John Wiley & Sons, 1997 (ISBN 0-471-97444-7).

A traditional description of the software life cycle, based on the well-known European Space Agency PSS-05 software engineering standards, is available as a book containing the standards more or less verbatim. It has clear descriptions of the basic activities needed during the user requirements and software specification phases. Its checklists, glossary, form templates, and tables of contents are especially useful.

Software Engineering Standards, C. Mazza *et al.*, Prentice-Hall, 1994 (ISBN 0-13-106568-8).

A practical guide to all aspects of requirements engineering on large industrial projects with a strong focus on process and the Capability Maturity Model (CMM) is

Effective Requirements Practices, Ralph R. Young, Addison-Wesley, 2001 (ISBN 0-201-70912-0).

A reflective, precise, and stimulating little book on many aspects of requirements by a famous practitioner is

Software Requirements and Specifications, a lexicon of practice, principles, and prejudices, Michael Jackson, ACM Press, Addison-Wesley, 1995 (ISBN 0-201-87712-0).

Jackson's most recent book looks in detail at the way that requirements have to span the divide between the world and the machine, describing the problem accurately enough to enable it to be solved:

Problem Frames, analyzing and structuring software development problems, Michael Jackson, Addison-Wesley, 2001 (ISBN 0-201-59627-X).

Scenarios and use cases

The best introduction to use cases, with many practical suggestions and simple templates, and a helpful checklist, is

Writing Effective Use Cases, Alistair Cockburn, Addison-Wesley, 2001 (ISBN 0-201-70225-8).

A thought-provoking book on the principles of organizing requirements, along with trenchant criticism of UML and many practical suggestions, is

Requirements Engineering and Rapid Development, an object-oriented approach, Ian Graham, ACM Press, Addison-Wesley, 1998 (ISBN 0-201-36047-0).

Although UML was not originally intended for user requirements, and use cases as originally introduced provided little structure, the use case has developed into the accepted way of describing scenarios for software, and is being adopted for other systems and for business process modeling. To be fair, it was introduced not for user requirements but for software specifications, in

Object-oriented Software Engineering – a use case driven approach, Ivar Jacobson *et al.*, Addison-Wesley, 1992 (ISBN 0-201-54435-0).

A collection of essays illustrating many different approaches to scenarios, including prototyping, human–computer interface design, and a short introduction to use cases by Jacobson, is

Scenario-Based Design, envisioning work and technology in system development, John M. Carroll (ed.), John Wiley & Sons, 1995 (ISBN 0-471-07659-7).

Much work on scenario techniques is published only in journals. There was a special issue of *IEEE Software* on requirements engineering in March/April 1998 (Volume 15 Number 2), containing a range of interesting articles on scenarios and other topics. A worthwhile paper on the practical use of scenarios is

Supporting Scenario-Based Requirements Engineering, Sutcliffe A.G., Maiden N.A.M., Minocha S. and Manuel D., 1998, IEEE Transactions on Software Engineering, 24(12), 1072–1088.

A completely different but very practical industrial take on specifying systems by considering the events that they need to handle, and the actions that they need to take to do so, is

Essential System Requirements, a practical guide to event-driven methods, Bill Wiley, Addison-Wesley, 2000 (ISBN 0-201-61606-8).

DOORS users can find a range of free tools that support modeling of scenarios and use cases on a website maintained by one of us (Alexander) at *Scenario Plus:* www.scenarioplus.org.uk

User involvement

Enid Mumford influenced engineering and business with her approach to the use of technology in the workplace. She introduced a method, ETHICS, which pioneered communication between users and system designers. A very readable short history of systems thinking with a strong emphasis on user participation is

Systems Design, ethical tools for ethical change, Enid Mumford, Macmillan, 1996 (ISBN 0-333-66946-0).

A serious but enjoyable book describing the failures of current systems approaches, and the need for user-centered development, from a telecoms perspective, is

The Trouble with Computers, usefulness, usability, and productivity, Thomas K. Landauer, MIT Press, 1995 (ISBN 0-262-12186-7).

Peter Checkland pioneered the concept of soft systems, and wrote several books discussing the problems of dealing with human issues in the context of engineering practice for "hard" systems. The book that established his reputation is

Systems Thinking, Systems Practice, Peter Checkland, John Wiley & Sons, 1981, reprinted 1999 with a "30-year retrospective" (ISBN 0-471-98606-2).

John Heron devised co-operative inquiry and has spent many years refining it. Perhaps the best summary of the approach and the theory behind it is his book

Co-operative Inquiry, John Heron, Sage, 1996 (ISBN 0-8039-7684-4).

Systems engineering

Books on systems engineering vary widely in what they believe the subject to be. The view embodied in this book is that it is an industrial process involving management, users, and developers, facing the challenge of organizing extremely complex developments. Stevens' book explains this view in detail:

Systems Engineering, coping with complexity, R. J. Stevens *et al.*, Prentice-Hall, 1998 (ISBN 0-13-095085-8).

One well-written and entertaining book which complements ours well is ostensibly about software but in fact covers many systems engineering issues in depth. It says little about writing requirements but much about the processes that use requirements throughout the systems engineering life cycle:

Managing Software Requirements, a unified approach, Dean Leffingwell and Don Widrig, Addison-Wesley, 1999 (ISBN 0-201-61593-2).

An inspiring book by one of the original architects of system thinking, showing how issues such as complexity, evolution, hierarchy, and planning interact to create systems, is

The Sciences of the Artificial, Herbert A. Simon, MIT Press, 1996 (ISBN 0-262-69191-4).

The definitive introduction to soft systems approaches, described with detailed case studies, has recently been reprinted with a "30-year retrospective" introduction, bringing it up to date and making it more approachable:

Soft Systems Methodology in Action, Peter Checkland and Jim Scholes, John Wiley & Sons, 1999 (ISBN 0-471-98605-4).

Index

Software Requirements
Styles and Techniques

Soren Lauesen

Most IT systems fail to meet expectations.
They don't meet business goals and don't
support users efficiently. Why? Because the
requirements didn't address the right
issues. Writing a good requirements specification doesn't take more time. This book
shows how it's done – many times faster
and many times smarter.

What are the highlights?

- Two complete real-life requirements
  specifications (the traditional and the
  fast approach) and examples from
  many others.
- Explanations of both traditional
  and fast approaches, and discussions of
  their strengths and weaknesses in different project types
  (tailor-made, COTS, and product development).
- Real-life illustrations of all types of requirements, stakeholder analysis, cost/benefit and
  other techniques to ensure that business goals are met.
- Proven methods for dealing with difficult or complex requirements, such as specifying ease-
  of-use, or dealing with 200 reports that might be needed because they are in the old system.

Who is it for?

Everyone involved in the software supply chain, from analysts and developers to end users,
will learn new techniques, benefit from requirements written by other specialists, and discover
successes and failures from other companies. Software suppliers will find ideas for helping customers and writing competitive proposals. Programmers and other developers will learn how
to express requirements without specifying technical details, and how to reduce risks when
developing a system. Students aspiring to IT careers will learn the theory and practice of
requirements engineering, and gain a strong foundation in case studies and projects.

Who is the author?

Soren Lauesen is currently professor at the IT-University of Copenhagen. He has worked in the
IT industry for 20 years and has been a professor at Copenhagen Business School for 15. He is
the co-founder of three educational and two industrial development organizations. His industry projects have encompassed compilers, operating systems, process control, temporal
databases, and software quality assurance. His research interests include human-computer
interaction, requirements specification, object-oriented design, quality assurance, marketing
and product development, and interaction between research and industry.

ISBN: 0 201 74570 4

Visit us on the world wide web at
www.it-minds.com
www.aw.com/cseng/